P9-CRR-078

THE SACRED JOURNEY

OTHER BOOKS BY FREDERICK BUECHNER

NONFICTION
The Magnificent Defeat
The Hungering Dark
The Alphabet of Grace
Wishful Thinking: A Theological ABC
The Faces of Jesus
Telling the Truth: The Gospel as Tragedy, Comedy and Fairy Tale
Peculiar Treasures: A Biblical Who's Who

FICTION
A Long Day's Dying
The Seasons' Difference
The Return of Ansel Gibbs
The Final Beast
The Entrance to Porlock
Lion Country
Open Heart
Love Feast
Treasure Hunt
The Book of Bebb
Godric

THE SACRED
JOURNEY

Frederick Buechner

1817

Harper & Row, Publishers, San Francisco

New York, Grand Rapids, Philadelphia, St. Louis
London, Singapore, Sydney, Tokyo, Toronto

Designer: Jim Mennick

Library of Congress Cataloging in Publication Data

Buechner, Frederick
   THE SACRED JOURNEY.

   1. Buechner, Frederick, 1926–. 2. Presbyterian
Church—Clergy—Biography. 3. Clergy—United States—
Biography. I. Title.
BX9225.B768A37 1982   285′.13 [B]   81-47843
ISBN 0-06-061158-8   AACR2

90 12 11

For Louis Patrick
and all the other saints,
remembered and forgotten, along the way

Contents

Introduction

ABOUT TEN years ago I gave a set of lectures at
Harvard in which I made the observation that all theol-
ogy, like all fiction, is at its heart autobiography, and that
what a theologian is doing essentially is examining as
honestly as he can the rough-and-tumble of his own experience with all its ups and downs, its mysteries and loose
ends, and expressing in logical, abstract terms the truths
about human life and about God that he believes he has
found implicit there. More as a novelist than as a theologian, more concretely than abstractly, I determined to try
to describe my own life as evocatively and candidly as I
could in the hope that such glimmers of theological truth
as I believed I had glimpsed in it would shine through my
description more or less on their own. It seemed to me
then, and seems to me still, that if God speaks to us at all
in this world, if God speaks anywhere, it is into our
personal lives that he speaks. Someone we love dies, say.
Some unforeseen act of kindness or cruelty touches the

heart or makes the blood run cold. We fail a friend, or a friend fails us, and we are appalled at the capacity we all of us have for estranging the very people in our lives we need the most. Or maybe nothing extraordinary happens at all—just one day following another, helter-skelter, in the manner of days. We sleep and dream. We wake. We work. We remember and forget. We have fun and are depressed. And into the thick of it, or out of the thick of it, at moments of even the most humdrum of our days, God speaks. But what do I mean by saying that God speaks?

I wrote these words at home on a hot, hazy summer day. On the wall behind me, an old banjo clock was tick-tocking the time away. Outside I could hear the twitter of swallows as they swooped in and out of the eaves of the barn. Every once in a while, in the distance, a rooster crowed, though it was well past sunup. Several rooms away, in another part of the house, two men were doing some carpentry. I could not make out what they were saying, but I was aware of the low rumble of their voices, the muffled sounds of their hammers, and the uneven lengths of silence in between. It was getting on toward noon, and from time to time my stomach growled as it went about its own obscure business which I neither understand nor want to. They were all of them random sounds without any apparent purpose or meaning, and yet as I paused to listen to them, I found myself hearing them with something more than just my ears to the point where they became in some way enormously meaningful. The swallows, the rooster, the workmen, my stomach, all with their elusive rhythms, their harmonies and disharmonies and counterpoint, became, as I listened, the sound of my own life speaking to me. Never had I heard just such a coming together of sounds before, and it is unlikely that I will ever hear them in just the same combination again. Their music was unique and unrepeatable and beyond describing in its freshness. I have no clear idea what the sounds meant or what my life was telling me. What does the song of a swallow mean? What is the muffled sound of a hammer trying to tell? And yet as I listened to those sounds, and listened with something more than just my hearing, I was moved by their inexpressible eloquence and suggestiveness, by the sense I had that they were a music rising up out of the mystery of not just my life, but of life itself. In much the same way, that is what I mean by saying that God speaks into or out of the thick of our days.

He speaks not just through the sounds we hear, of course, but through events in all their complexity and variety, through the harmonies and disharmonies and counterpoint of all that happens. As to the meaning of what he says, there are times that we are apt to think we know. Adolph Hitler dies a suicide in his bunker with the Third Reich going up in flames all around him, and what God is saying about the wages of sin seems clear enough. Or Albert Schweitzer renounces fame as a theologian and musician for a medical mission in Africa, where he ends up even more famous still as one of the great near-saints of Protestantism; and again we are tempted to see God's meaning as clarity itself. But what is God saying through a good man's suicide? What about the danger of the proclaimed saint's becoming a kind of religious prima donna as proud of his own humility as a peacock of its tail? What about sin itself as a means of grace? What about grace, when misappropriated and misunderstood, becoming an occasion for sin? To try to express in even the most insightful and theologically sophisticated terms the meaning of what God speaks through the events of our lives is as precarious a business as to try to express the meaning of the sound of rain on the roof or the spectacle of the setting sun. But I choose to believe that he speaks nonetheless, and the reason that his words are impossible to capture in human language is of course that they are ultimately always incarnate words. They are words fleshed out in the everydayness no less than in the crises of our own experience.

With all this in mind, I entitled those Harvard lectures *The Alphabet of Grace* in order to suggest that life itself can be thought of as an alphabet by which God graciously makes known his presence and purpose and power among us. Like the Hebrew alphabet, the alphabet of grace has no vowels, and in that sense his words to us are always veiled, subtle, cryptic, so that it is left to us to delve their meaning, to fill in the vowels, for ourselves by means of all the faith and imagination we can muster. God speaks to us in such a way, presumably, not because he chooses to be obscure but because, unlike a dictionary word whose meaning is fixed, the meaning of an incarnate word is the meaning it has for the one it is spoken to, the meaning that becomes clear and effective in our lives only when we ferret it out for ourselves. *Heilsgeschichte* is a more theological way of saying the same thing. Deep within history, as it gets itself written down in history books and newspapers, in the letters we write and in the diaries we keep, is sacred history, is God's purpose working itself out in the apparent purposelessness of human history and of our separate histories, is the history, in short, of the saving and losing of souls, including our own. A child is born. A friend is lost or found. Out of nowhere comes a sense of peace or foreboding. We are awakened by a dream. Out of the shadowy street comes a cry for help. We must learn to listen to the cock-crows and hammering and tick-tock of our lives for the holy and elusive word that is spoken to us out of their depths. It is the function of all great preaching, I think, and of all great art, to sharpen our hearing to precisely that end, and it was what I attempted in *The Alphabet of Grace.* I took a single, ordinary day of my life, and in describing the events of it—waking up, dressing, taking the children to school, working, and coming home again—I tried to suggest something of what I thought I had heard God saying.

That was ten years ago. By now my children have mostly grown up and mostly gone. I am not by a long shot entirely grown up myself, but I am ten years' worth of days older than I was then, and lots of things have happened to me, and I have had lots of time to listen to them happening. Also, since I passed the age of fifty, I have taken to looking back on my life as a whole more. I have looked through old letters and dug out old photographs. I have gone through twenty years' worth of old home movies. I have thought about the people I have known and the things that have happened that have, for better or worse, left the deepest mark on me. Like sitting there on the couch listening to the sounds of roosters, swallows, hammers, ticking clock, I have tried to make something out of the hidden alphabet of the years I have lived, to catch, beneath all the random sounds those years have made, a strain at least of their unique music. My interest in the past is not, I think, primarily nostalgic. Like everybody else, I rejoice in much of it and marvel at those moments when, less by effort than by grace, it comes to life again with extraordinary power and immediacy—vanished faces and voices, the feeling of what it was like to fall in love for the first time, of running as a child through the firefly dusk of summer, the fresh linen and cinnamon and servant-swept fragrance of my grandmother's house in Pennsylvania, the taste of snow, the stubbly touch of my father's good-night. But even if it were possible to return to those days, I would never choose to. What quickens my pulse now is the stretch ahead rather than the one behind, and it is mainly for some clue to where I am going that I search through where I have been, for some hint as to who I am becoming or failing to become that I delve into what used to be. I listen back to a time when nothing was much farther from my thoughts than God for an echo of the gutturals and sibilants and vowellessness by which I believe that even then God was addressing me out of my life as he addresses us all. And it is because I believe that, that I think of my life and of the lives of everyone who has ever lived, or will ever live, as not just journeys through time but as sacred journeys.

Ten years ago in those Harvard lectures, I tried to listen to a single day of my life in such a way. What I propose to do now is to try listening to my life as a whole, or at least to certain key moments of the first half of my life thus far, for whatever of meaning, of holiness, of God, there may be in it to hear. My assumption is that the story of any one of us is in some measure the story of us all.

For the reader, I suppose, it is like looking through someone else's photograph album. What holds you, if nothing else, is the possibility that somewhere among all those shots of people you never knew and places you never saw, you may come across something or someone you recognize. In fact—for more curious things have happened—even in a stranger's album, there is always the possibility that as the pages flip by, on one of them you may even catch a glimpse of yourself. Even if both of those fail, there is still a third possibility which is perhaps the happiest of them all, and that is that once I have put away my album for good, you may in the privacy of the heart take out the album of your own life and search it for the people and places you have loved and learned from yourself, and for those moments in the past —many of them half forgotten—through which you glimpsed, however dimly and fleetingly, the sacredness of your own journey.

I

Once Below a Time

HOW DO you tell the story of your life—of how you were born, and the world you were born into, and the world that was born in you? "Once upon a time," you might say because all beginnings have a legendary quality about them, a promise of magic, but Dylan Thomas uses a different phrase about his childhood which strikes me as a more accurate one. "Once below a time," he says in his poem "Fern Hill," meaning, I assume, that, for a child, time in the sense of something to measure and keep track of, time as the great circus parade of past, present, and future, cause and effect, has scarcely started yet and means little because for a child all time is by and large *now* time and apparently endless. What child, while summer is happening, bothers to think much that summer will end? What child, when snow is on the ground, stops to remember that not long ago the ground was snowless? It is by its content rather than its duration that a child knows time, by its quality rather than its quantity —happy times and sad times, the time the rabbit bit your finger, the time you had your first taste of bananas and cream, the time you were crying yourself to sleep when somebody came and lay down beside you in the dark for comfort. Childhood's time is Adam and Eve's time before they left the garden for good and from that time on divided everything into before and after. It is the time before God told them that the day would come when they would surely die with the result that from that point on they made clocks and calendars for counting their time out like money and never again lived through a day of their lives without being haunted somewhere in the depths of them by the knowledge that each day brought them closer to the end of their lives.

Once below a time, then, I was born into time neither knowing what it was nor much caring and yet, I suspect, seeing it more nearly for what it truly is than I have perhaps ever managed to see it since. Summers end, to be sure, and when the sun finally burns out like a match, they will end permanently; but be that as it may, it can never be otherwise than that there was a time when summers were. Come fire or flood, it can never be otherwise than that some fifty years ago, on some July or August day at dusk, I raced as a child through fireflies across a green lawn and in some way, with the insight of a child, sensed that that moment would never cease. What was true in my childhood belief that each of our times goes on forever was that once a moment has come into being, its having-beenness is beyond any power in heaven or earth, in life or in death, to touch. What I knew then, without knowing that I knew, was that to see the dusk, the fireflies, the green lawn, in their truth and fullness is to see them, as a child does, already clothed with timelessness, already freighted with all the aeons still to come during which they and everything else that ever was will continue eternally to be what has been— a part of the wholeness and truth of eternity itself.

And the people I knew as a child—my parents and grandparents, my brother, the nurses who came and went, the teachers and friends, the characters in books. I saw them all in much the same way as boundless. It never crossed my mind that there had been a time before they were or that there would ever come a time when they would be no longer. They were the Atlases who held the world on their shoulders—held my world anyway, held me—and their heads towered above the clouds. As with time, I had not yet acquired the fateful skill of standing off from them to weigh and measure. As I knew time for what it contained, I knew them for what they had it in them to give me or to withhold, knew them not for whoever they were in themselves, but for who they were for me. Mommy, Daddy, Grandma Buechner, Naya—the names they had were the names I gave them, and through these new names I gave them, I gave them also new selves to become—made my father a father, my mother a mother—and what they were apart from me, I no more knew or cared than I knew or cared what the world had been before I made my appearance in it or what the ocean was like when I was not there to feel it suck the sand out from beneath my bare feet. And the place where I started out during this once-below-a-time time was Eden, of course. One way or another it is where all of us start out, if we have any luck at all.

I had dominion then over all the earth and over every living thing that moves upon the earth. I saw the earth and its creatures not with the cool eye of the spectator, but with all the passion of a participant in whatever the extraordinary business is that we are all of us participating in, all of us in it together, as it is in all of us. There is no way to recapture fully the wonder and wildness of it. I knew trees before I knew what a tree was or thought I did, knew the cool rustle and darkness of them shot through with flashes of green sun. I knew weather of all kinds, and of all kinds loved rain best and always have. I would sit in a deckchair in it with a tarpaulin over me, hearing it drum on the canvas sunshade over my head, and loved it for leaving me snug and dry from its drenching, loved umbrellas and the oilskin smell of yellow sou'westers and slickers. There were pinwheel-colored beach umbrellas too that you could lay down on their sides, sheltering yourself among their shallow ribs against the stiff shore breeze that could do no more than whip a little stinging sand in around the edges until every once in a while a gust would get inside and send it cartwheeling crazily down the glistening flats to scatter nursemaids and bathers and sandpipers like chaff. The umbrellas were kept with pails and shovels and rope, old bathing caps and rubber bathing shoes, in a weathered chest that smelled musty and sweet and wooden inside, smelled of sand and summer and secrets and hemp. There were tomato worms, peagreen and fat, bedecked like floats in a Chinese New Year's parade, and a tiny scarlet bug no bigger than the head of a pin that I watched once move across the moonscape of a rock that I was playing hide-and-seek behind, knowing even then that I would never forget him for the rest of my days as indeed I never have, the meeting of that boy and that bug half a century ago, before time started.

As my father moved from job to job during the Great Depression of the thirties, we moved from place to place and house to house. In the section of Washington, D.C., called Georgetown, we had a brick-walled garden where I sat with a nurse named Mrs. Taylor, who said one day, "Now I am going to show you something that you have never seen before." Then she opened her mouth wide and sang out a single loud, clear note, and as she held it, her teeth dropped a full half an inch before my marveling eyes. She was right. I had never seen such a thing before.

This was the same Mrs. Taylor who, another time in that same garden, showed me a cut of raw beefsteak and, pointing to a small knot of white gristle somewhere toward the center, said, "That is the soul. Now you know what a soul looks like." She had a suitcase too, with a knife in it which she said had killed a Mexican, and she had something made out of glass that she said I was not old enough yet to see. She cut the pictures of things and the names of things out of magazines for me to paste in a scrapbook and taught me that way how to read and write when I was five. Then, after she put my brother and me to bed at night, she would lie down next to us in the dark and lead us in the same songs we always seemed to sing, one of them "The Spanish Cavalier" and another "The Old Rugged Cross," which as far as I can remember was the only hymn I ever heard as the child of non-church-going parents, although I had no idea what a hymn was or what a cross was or why it was something to sing about in the dark.

She was my mentor, my miracle-worker, and the mother of much that I was and in countless unrecognizable ways probably still am, yet I don't know where she came from or anything about her life apart from the few years of it that she spent with us. Nor do I know what became of her after she left, and there is a sadness in not knowing, in thinking of all the mothers and fathers we have all of us had who, for the little we remember them, might as well never have existed at all except for the deep and hidden ways in which they exist in us still. In any case, Mrs. Taylor was the one who vastly increased my dominion over the earth and its creatures by teaching me the art of naming them. It was not till years later that I learned what a fatal art that is because if, on the one hand, to name a thing is to be able to address it, to appropriate it, to have a way of understanding it, it is, on the other hand, to erect a barrier between yourself and it which only on the rarest and most inspired occasions are you ever able to surmount again. Now that, thanks to Mrs. Taylor, I can name a tree as a tree, what I see when I look at it is less what it actually is than simply the name I name it by. When I was a child, what I saw when I looked at a tree was something as naked in its mystery as I was naked in mine. Yet I thank her anyway. If she had not taught me the names, somebody else would have, and probably not half so well.

It was in Washington too that at this same time I was sick for the better part of a year with a glittering combination of pneumonia, tonsillitis, and pleurisy, and during the period that I was in bed, I lived, as much as I could be said to live anywhere, not in the United States of America but in the Land of Oz. One Oz book after another I read or had read to me until the world where animals can speak, and magic is common as grass, and no one dies, was so much more real to me than the world of my own room that if I had had occasion to be homesick then, it would have been Oz, not home, that I would have been homesick for as in a way I am homesick for it still.

I suppose it is partly because you read so much more slowly as a child that the books you come to then seem as endless as summer and richer, fuller, more inexhaustible than anything you are likely to read later on. The Shaggy Man with his magnet that made anybody who saw it love him and made him love anybody he saw. Queen Langwidere with her thirty interchangeable heads, one for each day of the month, and her roomful of mirrors in which she could admire their beauty as she tried them on one by one. The monster Quiberon, who guarded the Ozure Isles with their jeweled beaches and sapphire cliffs, and Ugu, the villainous shoemaker-magician, who lived in a wicker castle that he could make turn slowly upside down to the consternation of his enemies. They had life in them for me far beyond the scenes from their lives that L. Frank Baum and his successors chose to describe. I could picture them not just involved in other adventures that Baum himself never dreamed of, but going about their daily lives off-camera, so to speak —eating and sleeping and moving about with just as much plausibility and life as anybody I knew in real life, if not more. Reading an Oz book was like seeing a movie where the illusion of reality is so complete that, even beyond the doors of the set that are not opened, and around the bends of roads where your eye cannot see, you have utter faith that the world of the drama goes on with as much reality as the world itself.

For reasons that I can only guess at now, no one I came to know during that first year in Oz left a deeper mark on me than a plump, ebullient king named Rinkitink. He was a foolish man in many ways who laughed too much and talked too much and at moments of stress was apt to burst into unkingly tears; but beneath all that, he gave the impression of remarkable strength and resilience and courage even, a good man to have around when the chips were down. He and his young friend Prince Inga of Pingaree came into possession of three magic pearls—a blue one that conferred such strength that no power could resist it; a pink one that protected its owner from all dangers; and a pure white one that could speak words of great wisdom and helpfulness. "Never question the truth of what you fail to understand," the white pearl said when Rinkitink consulted it for the first time, "for the world is filled with wonders." It was great wisdom indeed, and has proved greatly helpful many times since.

Rinkitink was a very vulnerable man, silly and unstable in numberless ways, but in his fatness he seemed also somehow solid and substantial, eccentric and yet reliable with his slippered feet planted heavily on the ground and his heart in the right place. Like a tree that has been blown for years from so many directions by so many winds that none of them can ever quite blow it down, he seemed strong in his very vulnerability. In his capacity to laugh and weep at the drop of a hat and in general to make a fool of himself, he seemed wise with the wisdom of a child who sees better than his elders that the world is indeed something to laugh and weep about and who, more realistically than the rest of us, accepts his own foolishness as part of the givenness of things. Frightening and terrible adventures befall him in the course of Baum's book, but somehow he always manages to come riding out of them on the back of his faithful goat Bilbil. The world can wound him and scare the daylights out of him, but never, you feel, can it destroy him. It is only the world of the fairy tale to be sure, but nonetheless he has overcome that world, and I have remembered him with admiration and love ever since.

In different guises (though always fat) and under different names, Rinkitink has haunted me always. In gaiters and spectacles, he reappeared in my boyhood reading as Mr. Samuel Pickwick of *Pickwick Papers,* and in toga and laurel wreath as the Emperor Claudius in Robert Graves' *I, Claudius* and *Claudius the God.* When I was about fourteen, to jump ahead a few years, I met another version of him in the pages of G. K. Chesterton's *The Man Who Was Thursday,* where he appears as the character of Sunday, the huge, ebullient, antic leader of a group of supposed anarchists, who only at the end of that extraordinary fantasy turns out to have been also the policeman in the dark room who secretly signed them all up to do battle against anarchy. And a few years later still he turned up as the character of the whiskey priest in Graham Greene's novel *The Power and the Glory,* where what Greene fathomlessly conveys is that the power and glory of God are so overwhelming that they can shine forth into the world through even such a one as this seedy, alcoholic little failure of a man who thus, less by any virtue of his own than by the sheer power of grace within him, becomes a kind of saint at the end, just as Rinkitink the plump and absurd ends up vanquishing all the dark powers mustered against him; and as Mr. Pickwick bumbles his way through one misadventure after another to become one of the great heroes of English literature; and as Claudius the stammerer and reputed half-wit turns out to be one of the shrewdest and most effective of the Caesars; and as Sunday, that billowing, zany powerhouse of a man, reveals his true identity finally by saying, "I am the Sabbath. I am the Peace of God." Nothing was more remote from my thought at this period than theological speculation—except for Greene's, these books were all childhood or early boyhood reading—but certain patterns were set, certain rooms were made ready, so that when, years later, I came upon Saint Paul for the first time and heard him say, "God chose what is foolish in the world to shame the wise, God chose what is weak in the world to shame the strong, God chose what is low and despised in the world, even things that are not, to bring to nothing things that are," I had the feeling that I knew something of what he was talking about. Something of the divine comedy that we are all of us involved in. Something of grace.

I loved the rain as a child. I loved the sound of it on the leaves of trees and roofs and window panes and umbrellas and the feel of it on my face and bare legs. I loved the hiss of rubber tires on rainy streets and the flip-flop of windshield wipers. I loved the smell of wet grass and raincoats and the shaggy coats of dogs. A rainy day was a special day for me in a sense that no other kind of day was—a day when the ordinariness of things was suspended with ragged skies drifting to the color of pearl and dark streets turning to dark rivers of reflected light and even people transformed somehow as the rain drew them closer by giving them something to think about together, to take common shelter from, to complain of and joke about in ways that made them more like friends than it seemed to me they were on ordinary sunny days. But more than anything, I think, I loved rain for the power it had to make indoors seem snugger and safer and a place to find refuge in from everything outdoors that was un-home, unsafe. I loved rain for making home seem home more deeply, and I suspect that is why, from as far back as I can remember, I also loved those books I read and the people I met in them and the worlds they opened up to me. Like a house in the rain, books were havens of permanence and protection from whatever it was that as a child I needed protection from. Oz might be full of magic and danger, but even so it was safer than Washington was.

I remember, at the age of five or six, standing in the lobby of the Mayflower Hotel there one day when suddenly everybody around me was saying, "The President is coming, the President is coming," and starting to crowd around. Then slowly the doors of the main elevator rolled back, and there, framed in the opening, was the President himself with braces on his legs and one of his sons on either side of him, holding him up under the arms, and I remember realizing that if they had let him go, he would have crumpled to the floor like a doll. King Rinkitink would not have crumpled to the floor, but President Roosevelt would have crumpled because nowhere in Washington, as far as I then knew, was there a blue pearl to confer strength and a pink one for invulnerability and a white one with words wise and helpful enough to sustain him.

I suppose it was having no one house I had lived in

always that made the world seem so perilous and uncertain. Virtually every year of my life until I was fourteen, I lived in a different place, had different people to take care of me, went to a different school. The only house that remained constant was the one where my maternal grandparents lived in a suburb of Pittsburgh called East Liberty. It was big and white with a drawing room on one side of the central hall and a library on the other filled with marvelous books—lives of Napoleon and Cardinal Richelieu I remember especially, with pictures by the great French illustrator Job, and a Boutet de Monvel *Joan of Arc,* and some of the Andrew Lang fairy-tale books with their violent, crimson, blue covers stamped in gold—and a hearth broom carved with the face of a malevolent dwarf with the bristles for hair which struck such horror in me that my step-greatgrandmother let me lie with my head in her lap and an afghan over me to shut out the sight of it. There was a billiard room in the basement with a moosehead over the fireplace and high shelves full of yellow-backed French novels. There was a sleeping porch upstairs and my bachelor uncle's private quarters that smelled of shaving soap and damp towels and unimaginable wickedness. And in the bedrooms there were fireplaces that had little vertical asbestos grates that burned gas and made a lovely rippling sound when Ellen the maid lit them in the morning before we were up.

It was the one place in my childhood that we kept going back to, and for years I went back to it in dreams, to the third floor especially, where the servants' rooms and storage rooms were. There were doors up there that I was never quite brave enough to do more than peer through and mysteries up there that I never found heart enough to explore so that what I was up to in my dreams of going back to it, I suppose, was taking care of unfinished business, trying to find something that at the time I had somehow missed, like courage perhaps or an answer to questions that at the time I had not known how to ask. When Mrs. Taylor sang "The Old Rugged Cross" with us in the dark, among the words that she belted out with her teeth dropping half an inch in the process were the ones that go, "Then He'll call me someday to my home far away / Where His glory forever I'll share"; and for all I know, at the heart of my dreams about that home of my grandparents, so far away in time, was a sense that there was a home even farther away and fuller of mystery still and that, until I found it, I would be somehow homeless. In any case, apart from that one house on Woodland Road, home was not a place to me when I was a child. It was people.

How they do live on, those giants of our childhood, and how well they manage to take even death in their stride because although death can put an end to them right enough, it can never put an end to our relationship with them. Wherever or however else they may have come to life since, it is beyond a doubt that they live still in us. Memory is more than a looking back to a time that is no longer; it is a looking out into another kind of time altogether where everything that ever was continues not just to be, but to grow and change with the life that is in it still. The people we loved. The people who loved us. The people who, for good or ill, taught us things. Dead and gone though they may be, as we come to understand them in new ways, it is as though they come to understand us—and through them we come to understand ourselves—in new ways too. Who knows what "the communion of saints" means, but surely it means more than just that we are all of us haunted by ghosts because they are not ghosts, these people we once knew, not just echoes of voices that have years since ceased to speak, but saints in the sense that through them something of the power and richness of life itself not only touched us once long ago, but continues to touch us. They have their own business to get on with now, I assume—"increasing in knowledge and love of Thee," says the Book of Common Prayer, and moving "from strength to strength," which sounds like business enough for anybody—and one imagines all of us on this shore fading for them as they journey ahead toward whatever new shore may await them; but it is as if they carry something of us on their way as we assuredly carry something of them on ours. That is perhaps why to think of them is a matter not only of remembering them as they used to be but of seeing and hearing them as in some sense they are now. If they had things to say to us then, they have things to say to us now too, nor are they by any means always things we expect or the same things.

It is the way I used to see her on late Saturday afternoons in winter that I remember my Grandmother Buechner best. She sits in her overstuffed chair with the lamp behind her unlit, though New York City is turning gray through the window. On the sill at her elbow, her squat little Philco is playing Wagner. She knows the libretto by heart as she also knows by heart how to crochet in the dusk with her silk and scissors lying on the great shelf of her bosom. Wotan is singing farewell to Brünn-hilde—*"Leb' wohl, du kühnes, herrliches Kind! Du meines Herzens heiliger Stolz"*— while twelve stories down on Park Avenue, taxi horns echo the music's grieving. "Farewell, my brave and beautiful child, the life and light of my heart," sings Wotan as, ringed round with fire, Brünnhilde sinks into an enchanted sleep. *Leb' wohl.* Then Rosa the maid comes in with her *Essen ist fertig, Frau Büchner* to announce dinner, and my grandmother heaves her great weight out of her chair and with the aid of her stick and my arm makes her way to the dining room table of cold chicken, radishes, rye bread, and *lebkuchen* left over from Christmas. She talks of the *tanten* —how Tante Anna said of her, "Louise always tells me I'm naive, but what she means is I'm stupid," and of how Tante Anna phoned not long before to say that she had fallen and broken the bone in her eye. "The bone in her eye!" my grandmother says and laughs till out of her own eyes the tears roll down.

She talks of her father, Hermann Balthazar Scharmann, and of how walking back from luncheon at Lüchows, he would keep hurling his cane yards ahead on the pavement, pedestrians be damned, and then pick it up without breaking his stride to keep himself trim. "I'm too old," my grandmother says. "Somebody should shoot me," but of course we none of us dared. Instead we would bring her presents on her birthday, which Heaven help us if we forgot, and she would sit there in her chair by the window refusing to open them. "Whatever they are," she says, "I know I'm not going to like them."

She was the rich one of my two grandmothers, the

holder of the purse strings. She could be an unholy terror, and when the terror was at its unholiest, Rosa would answer the doorbell with the single word *Grenma,* her hands in the air and her eyes rolled heavenward. My grandmother spoke her mind with terrible honesty, in German to Rosa and in English to the rest of us. But if her wrath burned hot, it also burned quick and was gone in a devastating flash. She never smoldered. And it was the same with her grief. Suddenly her voice would tremble, her eyes brim, over some ancient hurt, some remembered loss or failure. She never submerged her feelings but rode them like a great wave just the way, as a child, I often saw her ride the real waves too, swimming out to the barrels through the high Long Island surf as fat as Rinkitink but bobbing like a great cork, unsinkable, ocean-proof. Then back to the big shingled summer house by the canal, where ducks quacked for breadcrumbs and bees buzzed among the honeysuckle, and all through the house there were bowls of flowers—black-eyed Susans, wild roses, cattails—and cold crab in the ice box, cold beer, and lemonade in crockery pitchers, a mocha torte with ground almonds in it that took two days to make. My grandmother played croquet with her tennis-playing sons and golf-playing daughter, held her mallet one-handed and off to the side as she had learned to from the years when she needed that one hand free to gather up the long skirts of her girlhood. Her tow-headed grandchildren played hide-and-seek on the lawn as the dusk deepened and my grandfather poured out the evening martinis on the veranda.

He was sometimes mistaken for the British actor C. Aubrey Smith on his travels, my grandfather, and when

people came up to ask for his autograph, he always
obliged them but always signed his own name. There was
a marble bust of Venus de Milo in the living room in
New York, and I remember as a child being there alone
with him once as he sat in his chair across from my
grandmother's with his glass in his hand. I felt his eye
upon me, and shy of him, tongue-tied, not knowing what
else to do, I wandered over to where the bust stood and,
with no sense of what I was about, reached up and
touched one of the cool, white breasts. I can hear his
short, dry laugh still—as short and dry as his martini and
wickeder. It was the future that I had touched without
knowing it, but he knew it. The day would come. The
curtain would rise. I was humiliated. His moustache was
damp with gin. Not a word was spoken. It was a moment.

"Oh, it was so many years ago," my grandmother
says, "and there were so many of you then, all four of my
children alive still, and how little I dreamed then the
terrible things that—" and suddenly she is dabbing at her
eye, her voice in a tremble. "Never mind," she says.
"Tears are an old Scharmann custom."

But of course she *had* dreamed them—the terrible
things—maybe not the ones that actually happened when
their time came, but others no less terrible and even
more so for all I know. All her life she was a worrier,
brooding like a hen over terrors to come almost as
though to hatch them out into reality would be a kind of
relief because there at least she could come to some sort
of terms with them as in her dark dreams she could not.
So when they did come—her husband and two of her
sons falling like dominoes before their time, a fortune all
but lost—she was ready for them in her way, found

strength somewhere for surviving them. She would never have said that it was in God that she found it. If she spoke of God at all, it was always as *le bon Dieu* with an obscure little smile on her lips, a smile that was an only half satiric little curtsy in the direction of a belief which she herself did not hold but was perhaps not altogether willing to dismiss out of hand either any more than she would have dismissed it out of hand if a child had said he believed in fairies or the Man in the Moon. Who could tell, after all? But from her German forebears—free-thinkers and radicals who had come to this country during the troubles of 1848—the strongest faith she inherited was faith in hard work, in being careful with your money, in families staying together through thick and thin even unto the third and fourth generation of kaffee-klatsching cousins, in the strength that comes with facing even what is vastly stronger than yourself.

Sayings of her father, old Hermann Scharmann, came easily to her lips. "Never put on your bathing suit without going in the water," he said. He was a tyrant, a tycoon, a self-made man who through breweries and real estate was able to leave each of his many children a grand piano and more than money enough never to starve. As a child he had gone with his parents to California in the Gold Rush, his mother and a baby sister dying on the way to be buried by a river at Christmas time, and the rest of them barely able to pan enough gold to keep themselves alive before they finally limped back to Brooklyn where they had started from. My great-grandfather liked being thought of as a Forty-niner, even though he was only a child at the time, and when he had his father's memoirs of the trip privately printed many years later, it was his own picture, not his father's, that he had printed as the frontispiece. "Never put anything off because of the weather," he said, and from the look of his picture—those bulging eyes, those jowls, that fierce goatee—it is easier to imagine the weather's putting something off because of him.

Like her father, my grandmother had little patience with weakness, softness, sickness. Even gentleness made her uncomfortable, I think—tender-hearted people who from fear of giving pain, or just from fear of her, hung back from speaking their minds the way she spoke hers, let the Devil take the hindmost. Only once can I remember her having been gentle in her way, responding to gentleness gently. It was a day or two after the death of her eldest son, my father. We must have gone to her apartment for lunch, my mother, brother, and I, and Grandma and my mother had lingered over their coffee, talking to each other about the young man whose love they had fought each other for over the years. The dining room doors were open, and their voices drifted out with the smell of their coffee to where my brother and I were waiting for it to be time to go home to whatever home was just then. "With malice toward none," we heard my mother say. "With charity for all," and then the murmur of my grandmother's voice more terrible in its gentleness than it had ever been in its wrath, then the tinkle of a silver spoon against a china cup as those two old adversaries found it possible for perhaps the only time in their lives to weep together over a life that neither of them had had whatever it might have taken in the way of gentleness or strength to save.

But she came out of it in the end on the far side of

tears, and my clearest memory of her is sitting dry-eyed
by the same window, in that same chair, with that same
small radio at her elbow, and one of the bedspreads that
she was always crocheting out of linen thread spread out
over her knees. It is Wagner again, only *Die Götterdämmerung* this time. It is the twilight of the gods. Valhalla
is about to go up in flames. My grandmother sits there,
the oldest living survivor. Like a rock at the edge of the
sea, she bears the marks of the storm. Sharp edges have
been pounded smooth. Parts have crumbled away altogether because though you can ignore the weather, you
cannot alter it. But the rock still stands, bird-spattered
and barnacled, a fixed point for the rest of us to steer
clear of in one sense and to steer by in another, to get our
bearings by. "Your father was gentle," she says. "The
world is not gentle." It is less Siegfried suddenly than my
father who lies there on his funeral pyre. *"Der Reinste war
er . . . laut'rer als er liebte kein And'rer,"* Brünnhilde sings
with the burning torch in her hand. "He was the truest
. . . no other loved so truly." But then, *"Trog keiner wie
er!"* "None broke like him!" she cries—whoever it is
lying there broken, broke, heart-broken, and heart-
breaking as she touches his pyre with her torch. The little
Philco's tubes rattle like teeth as the music flashes and
swells and then dwindles to a single flute. The crochet
hook is still.

My grandmother's jokes tended to have something
medieval about them—heavy, wooden, with little art but
made to do hard service. There was this preacher once,
she says, preaching his sermon from his pulpit in his long
black gown. It was such a hot day that he had put nothing
on but the gown that morning and was as naked under-

neath as the day he was born. He got so wrought up over his sermon and was pounding and stomping around so hard up there that suddenly the platform gave way beneath him and he was pitched almost into the laps of his congregation with his black gown tossed up over his head. "May anyone who looks be struck blind!" he yelled out, and the whole congregation dutifully clapped their hands to their eyes with the exception of one old woman who let two fingers slip apart just enough for a chink to peer through. "I'll risk one eye," she said.

My grandmother was the old woman, of course. No doom she ever dreamed can have been as dark as the one that finally overtook her, but with no faith to fall back on, other than such faith as she had in herself and such faith as she had left in what was left of her family, and with no God except *le bon Dieu,* whoever and whatever he was, if indeed he was anywhere at all, she never pretended that things were other than they were. She never armed herself against the world with bitterness or capitulated to it with despair. She looked at it bare, and she looked at it hard, and for a wonder she was never blinded. "Farewell," sings Wotan, "my brave and beautiful child."

As for me as a child, I was no braver than I was beautiful, nor, up to the age of ten, did I have anything out of the ordinary to be brave about. But at the same time, for a child—especially a bookish, rain-loving, inward-looking child—even the ordinary can at times require bravery enough. The hearth broom with the face of a malevolent dwarf. The servant's child, floating face down in the canal in front of the shingled house one morning—fished out and resuscitated, but appalling,

shameful somehow, as it lay there puddling the weathered planks of the dock with the water that ran from its
nose and mouth as the breath came rattling back. The
circus horse, white as milk and brilliantly bridled, balking
outside the great tent with a man beating it about the face
and eyes with a stick. The green frog that some cousins
and I tossed back and forth by one of its legs like a green
toy until at last it broke like a toy and the slippery life
came spilling out. The unexplored rooms on the third
floor, and the new nurse who did not understand her
instructions and thus did not know that it was all right for
my brother and me to stay up an hour or so later to dye
Easter eggs, but packed us off to bed at the usual time
where we lay in the dark aghast at the sudden knowledge
that much of the time we lived at the sufferance of strangers.

But if strangers and strange sights can shake the world
of children, it takes the people they know and love best
to pull it out from under them like a chair. Into the same
Georgetown garden where Mrs. Taylor showed me the
tough, white gristle of a soul, my other grandmother
came one day. Naya was the name I had given her for
reasons long since lost to history. She was as different
from Grandma Buechner as a lamp to read by is different
from the twilight of the gods. She was a superb solver of
crossword puzzles and a reader of French novels. She
smoked cigarettes in white paper holders and watched
the world go by. She played wistful tunes with one finger
on a Steinway grand. She held me enraptured by tales of
the past, evoking in dazzlingly spoken paragraphs a
whole world of Dickensian freaks, relations and friends,
like adopted cousin Nelly Dunbar, with her oiled ring-

lets and Armenian blood, who would filch pink soap
from the family linen closet and peddle it on street corners; and Tante Elise Golay, who carried a watered silk
reticule to restaurants so she would have something to
empty the sugar bowl into when the meal was through;
and Naya's step-grandfather, Amasa Barret, who was
blind as a bat and told her—when as a child she asked him
what the name *Amasa* meant—that what it meant was "a
burden," and she could have bitten out her tongue. If
Grandma Buechner was a rock with the rough seas of her
life all but inundating her at times and yet immovable,
impermeable, intractable to the end, then Naya was the
old gray gull who rode it all out on the skin of the storm.
The waves might rise like Everest above her or sink like
the Valley of the Shadow beneath, but with her back to
the wind and her wings tucked tight, Naya rarely ruffled
so much as a feather. I see her knitting a scarf in a wicker
peacock chair with the Blue Ridge mountains blue behind her, or under a beach umbrella in pleated white
linen with her brave old Indian eyes on the far horizon,
or, when she was well into her nineties, writing, after we
had taken our first child to see her for the first time, "It
was a noble deed to make the long journey down here,
and the joy of seeing you two and your bewitching little
fairy daughter more than compensates me for the igno-
miny of substituting an old crone in a dark little room for
the Naya of legend."

In any case, of all the giants who held up my world,
Naya was perhaps chief, and when I knew she was coming to Georgetown for a visit that day, I wanted to greet
her properly. So what I did at the age of six was prepare
her a feast. All I could find in the icebox that seemed

suitable were some cold string beans that had seen better days with the butter on them long since gone to wax, and they were what I brought out to her in that fateful garden. I do not remember what she said then exactly, but it was an aside spoken to my parents or whatever grown-ups happened to be around to the effect that she did not usually eat much at three o'clock in the afternoon or whatever it was, let alone the cold string beans of another age, but that she would see what she could do for propriety's sake. Whatever it was, she said it drily, wittily, the way she said everything, never dreaming for a moment that I would either hear or understand, but I did hear, and what I came to understand for the first time in my life, I suspect—why else should I remember it?—was that the people you love have two sides to them. One is the side they love you back with, and the other is the side that, even when they do not mean to, they can sting you with like a wasp. It was the first ominous scratching in the walls, the first telltale crack in the foundation of the one home which perhaps any child has when you come right down to it, and that is the people he loves.

There were other cracks, of course. My brother and I had misbehaved at lunch for days, and at last, for the sake of having a peaceful meal by herself for once, my mother dressed up in a coat of my father's and one of his hats and had word sent up to us that a little old man had come to eat that day. So we stayed upstairs, needless to say, too timid to think of lunching with a stranger, and I remember looking down through the bannister and seeing at the dining-room table somebody who was both a little old man yet somehow also my mother; and again what had always seemed solid as a rock showed signs of cracking in two. Or the time my father was sick in bed for a day or two. That was all it took: my father sick, on whose health the foundations of the world were based; my father in bed when I knew that unless he stayed on his feet, the winds would die and the crops fail. Or, later on, my father coming in to say good-night and standing there at the foot of our beds with his hands on his hips and his face clammy and gray as he threw back his head and laughed in a way that made me know as surely as I knew anything that something had gone terribly wrong with his laughter. Something had gotten broken in it. Something in it was in danger of breaking him, breaking all of us. And the time he wanted the keys to the car, and my mother gave them to me and told me that he had had too much to drink and not to let him know where they were, no matter what, so that I lay in my bed with my pillow over my head and made no reply to his endless pleading because I could think of no reply that I could possibly make.

I no longer know what my father looked like, it has been so long since I saw him last, and have only photographs to remember his face by—a young man in a sailor's uniform, or sitting behind a desk in his first office, or lying in the sand in his swimming trunks and striped jersey top. But from somewhere deeper within myself than memory, and from what I have been able to find out over the years from people who knew him much longer and better than I, I can still summon up something of the feel of who he was. He was a gentle man, as my grandmother said, handsome and conscientious and kind. He was a strong swimmer who played water polo at college, and a good dancer, and could go nowhere, the family joke was, without running into at least six friends. He knew Zelda and Scott Fitzgerald from his Princeton days and knew waiters and barbers by their first names. People I doubt he would have remembered remember him still. As the oldest of four children, he was the one who shepherded the others through Central Park to school and from the start seems to have been given responsibilities beyond his years. Even in pictures of him as a small boy, he looks harried, seldom if ever smiling, as though he knew that as soon as the shutter snapped, it would all begin again—my grandmother saddling him with more, I suspect, than a small boy's share of her own dark burdens, his younger brothers and sister looking to him for some kind of strength, some kind of stability, which he must have had to dig deep into himself to find, having barely enough at that age, I can only imagine, to get by on himself. And then when he got married, and his two sons were born, and the crash of '29 came, there was a whole new set of things to be harried by as he moved from job to job and place to place, always bent on doing better by us, establishing us on some surer, more becoming ground.

He worked long hours and he worked hard at whatever minor executive job he happened to have at the time, but on weekends at least he found time to be a father. In an inlet full of jellyfish that stung, he taught me how to swim. He taught me how to ride a bike by running alongside with his hand on the handlebars till I started to get the hang of it, then taking his hand away and letting me roll along on my own till I wobbled finally into a hedge but knew how to do it from that day on. When at the age of nine or so I asked a pretty girl named

Virginia with shampoo-smelling hair to go to the movies with me (it was Eddie Cantor in *Roman Scandals*), he drove me to pick her up and explained on the way that she would probably keep us waiting a little because that was what pretty girls did, and he was right. When he came to say good-night, he would give my brother Jamie and me what he called a "hard kiss," which was all sandpapery whiskers and snorts and struggle. I remember sitting in the back seat of a car, with him and my mother up front, singing songs like "Me and My Shadow" and "That's My Weakness Now," remember eating dark Swiss chocolate and salty French bread with him on the long drives he took us on sometimes, remember one winter drive back over the Allegheny mountains from Pittsburgh when it was so cold that he gave the only blanket there was to us in the back seat and had to stuff newspaper under his coat to keep warm himself. I remember seeing the movie of *Green Pastures* with him— the great fish-fry in Heaven with De Lawd and his black angels—and driving down to the Quogue beach afterwards to see the moon rise like an angel over the incoming tide.

These were the bright times, the happy once-below-a-time times, but for a child even the bright times have, like the moon, their dark side too; and even below the time when time starts, the time to come can still cast a shadow. Any house where my father and mother were was home to me, but for that very reason, whenever they left—even for a day, even for an evening—it was home no longer but a house with walls as frail as paper and a roof as fragile as glass. My fear was that they would never come back.

I knew nothing more of death then than what I had learned of it from the slippery green frog, and nothing more of darkness than the night. I had never lost anything that I was not sure would be replaced if I really needed it by the people I loved, and I had never been hurt beyond the power of a word of comfort to heal. But whenever my father and mother left, taking home with them, I knew that hurt, loss, darkness, death could flatten that house in seconds. And to a degree that I had no way of knowing, and in ways that I could not possibly foresee, I was right.

II

Once Upon a Time

ON A SATURDAY in late fall, my brother and I woke up around sunrise. I was ten and he not quite eight, and once we were awake, there was no going back to sleep again because immediately all the excitement of the day that was about to be burst in upon us like the sun itself, and we could not conceivably have closed our eyes on it. Our mother and father were going to take us to a football game, and although we were not particularly interested in the game, we were desperately interested in being taken. Grandma Buechner had come down from the city to go with us and was asleep in another room. Our parents presumably were also asleep, and so were the black couple who worked for us, downstairs in a room off the kitchen. It was much too early to get up, so just as on Christmas morning when you wake up too early to start opening the presents, we amused ourselves as best we could till the rest of the house got moving and it came time to start opening the present of this new and most promising day. We had a roulette wheel, of all things—

black and glittery with a chromium spindle at the hub which it took only the slightest twirl to set spinning and the little ball skittering clickety-click around the rim until the wheel slowed down enough for it to settle into one of the niches and ride out the rest of the spin in silence.

We had a green felt cloth with the numbers and colors marked on it and a box of red, white, and blue poker chips; and all of this we had spread out on the foot of one of our beds, playing with it, when something happened that at the moment neither of us more than half noticed because it was such an ordinary thing in a way, set next to all the extraordinary things that we had reason to believe were going to happen as soon as the day got going. What happened was that our bedroom door opened a little, and somebody looked in on us. It was our father. Later on, we could not remember anything more about it than that, even when we finally got around to pooling our memories of it, which was not until many years later.

If he said anything to us, or if we said anything to him, we neither of us have ever been able to remember it. He could have been either dressed or still in his pajamas for all we noticed. There was apparently nothing about his appearance or about what he said or did that made us look twice at him. There was nothing to suggest that he opened the door for any reason other than just to check on us as he passed by on his way to the bathroom or wherever else we might have thought he was going that early on a Saturday morning, if either of us had bothered to think about it at all. I have no idea how long he stood there looking at us. A few seconds? A few minutes? Did he smile, make a face, wave his hand? I have no idea. All

I know is that after a while, he disappeared, closing the door behind him, and we went on playing with our wheel as I assume we had kept on playing with it right along because there was nothing our father had said or done or seemed to want that made us stop. Clickety clickety click. Now this number, now that. On one spin we could be rich as Croesus. On the next we could lose our shirts.

How long it was from the moment he closed that door to the moment we opened it, I no longer have any way of knowing, but the interlude can stand in a way for my whole childhood up till then and for everybody else's too, I suppose: childhood as a waiting for you do not know just what and living, as you live in dreams, with little or no sense of sequence or consequence or measurable time. And that moment was also the last of my childhood because, when I opened the door again, measurable time was, among other things, what I opened it on. The click of the latch as I turned the knob was the first tick of the clock that measures everything into before and after, and at that exact moment my once-below-a-time ended and my once-upon-a-time began. From that moment to this I have ridden on time's back as a man rides a horse, knowing fully that the day will come when my ride will end and my time will end and all that I am and all that I have will end with them. Up till then the house had been still. Then, muffled by the closed door, there was a shout from downstairs. It was the husband of the black couple. His voice was fruity and hollow with something I had never heard in it before. I opened the door.

All over the house doors opened, upstairs and down. My grandmother loomed fierce and terrified in the hallway, her nightgown billowing around her, white and stiff as a sail, her hair down her back. There was a blue haze in the air, faintly bitter and stifling. In what I remember still as a kind of crazy parody of excitement, I grabbed hold of the newel post at the top of the stairs and swung myself around it. "Something terrible has happened!" my grandmother said. She told us to go back to our room. We went back. We looked out the window.

Down below was the gravel drive, the garage with its doors flung wide open and the same blue haze thick inside it and drifting out into the crisp autumn day. I had the sense that my brother and I were looking down from a height many times greater than just the height of the second story of our house. In gray slacks and a maroon sweater, our father was lying in the driveway on his back. By now my mother and grandmother were with him, both in their nightgowns still, barefoot, their hair uncombed. Each had taken one of his legs and was working it up and down like the handle of a pump, but whatever this was supposed to accomplish, it accomplished nothing as far as we could see. A few neighbors had gathered at the upper end of the drive, and my brother and I were there with them, neither knowing how we got there nor daring to go any farther.

Nobody spoke. A car careened up and braked sharp with a spray of gravel. A doctor got out. He was wearing a fedora and glasses. He ran down the driveway with his bag in his hand. He knelt. I remember the black man who had roused us sitting somewhere with his head in his hands. I remember the dachshund we had wagging his tail. After a time the doctor came back up the drive, his tread noisy on the gravel. The question the neighbors asked him they asked without words, and without a word the doctor answered them. He barely shook his head. It was not for several days that a note was found. It was written in pencil on the last page of *Gone with the Wind,* which had been published that year, 1936, and it was addressed to my mother. "I adore and love you," it said, "and am no good. . . . Give Freddy my watch. Give Jamie my pearl pin. I give you all my love."

God speaks to us through our lives, we often too easily say. *Something* speaks anyway, spells out some sort of godly or godforsaken meaning to us through the alphabet of our years, but often it takes many years and many further spellings out before we start to glimpse, or think we do, a little of what that meaning is. Even then we glimpse it only dimly, like the first trace of dawn on the rim of night, and even then it is a meaning that we cannot fix and be sure of once and for all because it is always incarnate meaning and thus as alive and changing as we are ourselves alive and changing.

A child takes life as it comes because he has no other way of taking it. The world had come to an end that Saturday morning, but each time we had moved to another place, I had seen a world come to an end, and there had always been another world to replace it. When somebody you love dies, Mark Twain said, it is like when your house burns down; it isn't for years that you realize the full extent of your loss. For me it was longer than for most, if indeed I have realized it fully even yet, and in the meanwhile the loss came to get buried so deep in me that after a time I scarcely ever took it out to look at it at all, let alone to speak of it. If ever anybody asked me how my father died, I would say heart trouble. That seemed at least a version of the truth. He had had a heart. It had been troubled. I remembered how his laughter toward the end had rung like a cracked bell. I remembered how when he opened the bedroom door, he had not said good-bye to us in any way that we understood. I remembered what he had written on the last page of the book he had been reading.

And then by grace or by luck or by some cool, child's skill for withdrawing from anything too sharp or puzzling to deal with, I stopped remembering so almost completely to remember at all that when, a year or so later, I came upon my brother crying one day all by himself in his room, I was stopped dead in my tracks. Why was he crying? When I prodded him into telling me that he was crying about something that he would not name but said only had happened a long time ago, I finally knew what he meant, and I can recapture still my astonishment that, for him, a wound was still open that for me, or so I thought, had long since closed. And in addition to the astonishment, there was also a shadow of guilt. It was guilt not only that I had no tears like his to cry with but that if, no less than he, I had also lost more than I yet knew, I had also, although admittedly at an exorbitant price, made a sort of giddy, tragic, but quite measurable little gain. While my father lived, I was the heir apparent, the crown prince. Now I was not only king, but king in a place that, except for his death, I would probably never have known except in dreams. What I mean is that the place we moved to soon after he died—and it was there that my brother cried, in a house the color of smoked salmon overhanging a harbor of turquoise and ultramarine—was the Land of Oz.

No place I have ever been to since—no matter how remote, no matter how strange and lovely—can match the loveliness of the Bermuda islands as they still existed when I first saw them. There were no cars there in those days, none of the sounds or smells of combustion engines of any kind which have become so much a part of the world we live in that it is hardly possible any more to imagine either the world or our lives without them. The world was quieter and statelier without them, the distances greener and greater. There were only horses and carriages there then—Victorias mostly with their hooded, perambulator tops that could be put up if it rained, and slim English bicycles with bells and baskets, and a narrow-gauge Toonerville Trolley of a railway with wicker armchairs for seats that rattled through pawpaws and banana palms, over high trestles that swayed in the wind across inlets and coves from one end of the fishhook-shaped island to the other no faster, it seemed, than a boy could run. There were fields of lilies, hedges of oleander and hibiscus, passion flowers, moonflowers, and always the small, bent cedars that grew everywhere and whose fragrance enchanted the air you breathed together with the fragrance of horses, the sea, the faint sweetness of kerosene that Bermudians burned in those days when the evenings turned cool.

The houses were sky blue and rose, lemon yellow and lavender and pastel green, all with their blinding white roofs stepped to catch the rain because rain was all the water there was in Bermuda. You drank rain. You bathed in rain. You watched rain move in slow, sad curtains across the harbor where our house was, heard the soft hiss of its advance. It would come up out of nowhere and stop as suddenly, the porous coral roads drying in minutes—the chalky, damp smell of their drying. There were pale pink coral beaches turning to amber in the shallows, then shading off into Gulf Stream greens and purples and deep-sea blue. There were angel fish off our terrace, goggle-eyed squirrel fish, and sergeant majors, striped bumblebee yellow and black. There was a small, battered ferry called *The Dragon* that chugged you across to Hamilton for sixpence with its stern almost awash under a load of bikes. There were the great *Monarch* and the great *Queen,* which on alternate weeks slipped silent as ghosts through the narrows at daybreak, then foghorned, breathy and hoarse, as they started to dock. There was an eccentric with a golden brown beard and hair that grew down to his shoulders who used to hang around the custom sheds with a faraway look in his eyes and was always there by the gangplank when the Furness ships came in, watching the passengers as they got off one by one. Some said that he was looking for a woman who had deserted him, or a lost friend, a lost child, but he himself never told, or even told his name, so Jesus was what people called him because of his long hair and beard, I suppose, or the way he searched all the faces that passed him by. And there were the long-tailed Bermuda gulls.

Grandma Buechner was against our going, and with reason. It was the same kind of extravagance that had so weighed down my father, she said. It was a frivolous place to go at a grave time. It was no place to raise boys. It was escape. "You should stay and face reality," she wrote my mother, and old Hermann Scharmann, puffing a cigar on Millionaire's Row at Sheepshead Bay, would have nodded agreement if he had not been some fifteen years dead by then and, like his cigar, gone long since to ash. Reality was like the bad weather that you did not put things off because of, or seek refuge from in the Land of Oz. Reality was what the old woman in the joke peered out at through her fingers even though she knew the sight of it might strike her blind.

And my grandmother was right, of course—right in a hundred ways and wrong in as many others. She was right that reality can be harsh and that you shut your eyes to it only at your peril because if you do not face up to the enemy in all his dark power, then the enemy will come up from behind some dark day and destroy you while you are facing the other way. Maybe, if we had stayed home as she did, and wept for my father there, we might have become the stronger for it as certainly she became stronger herself because in her chair by the window she stared her doom straight in the eye until somehow she finally managed to stare it down altogether to emerge doom-proof at last with even her mirth intact like the soft, lyric passage that *Götterdämmerung* ends with after all the orchestral *sturm und drang* of Valhalla in flames. Who knows what we might have become? But she was also wrong. *Le bon Dieu,* she would say with that faint little smile, half ironic, half wistful, and if her smile never quite dismissed *le bon Dieu* himself, what I think it did dismiss was anything like the serious possibility that through flaws and fissures in the bedrock harshness of things, there wells up from time to time, out of a deeper substratum of reality still, a kind of crazy, holy grace.

"You should stay and face reality," she wrote, and in terms of what was humanly best, this was perhaps the soundest advice she could have given us: that we should stay and, through sheer Scharmann endurance, will, courage, put our lives back together by becoming as strong as she was herself. But when it comes to putting broken lives back together—when it comes, in religious terms, to the saving of souls—the human best tends to be at odds with the holy best. To do for yourself the best that you have it in you to do—to grit your teeth and clench your fists in order to survive the world at its harshest and worst—is, by that very act, to be unable to let something be done for you and in you that is more wonderful still. The trouble with steeling yourself against the harshness of reality is that the same steel that secures your life against being destroyed secures your life also against being opened up and transformed by the holy power that life itself comes from. You can survive on your own. You can grow strong on your own. You can even prevail on your own. But you cannot become human on your own. Surely that is why, in Jesus' sad joke, the rich man has as hard a time getting into Paradise as that camel through the needle's eye because with his credit card in his pocket, the rich man is so effective at getting for himself everything he needs that he does not see that what he needs more than anything else in the world can be had only as a gift. He does not see that the one thing a clenched fist cannot do is accept, even from *le bon Dieu* himself, a helping hand.

My mother took us to Bermuda, of all places, for no motive more profound than simply to get away from things for a while as my grandmother rightly saw; but to get away *from* is also to get away *to,* and that implausible island where we went within a month or two of my father's death turned out to be a place where healing could happen in a way that perhaps would not have been possible anywhere else and to a degree that—even with all the endurance, will, courage we might have been able to muster had we stayed—I do not think we could ever have achieved on our own.

Nazism was on the rise in Germany, and I remember being taken to see the newsreels of Hitler in his glory at the Berlin Olympics. The fall of Austria and the Munich pact were less than a year away, and the world was bumbling toward war. But all of this was not the world I lived in because, although time had begun for me with the shout from downstairs and the opening of the door, the outward, public history of our times seemed as remote to me then as in many ways it seems to me still. My world was twenty-five miles long, give or take, and some three miles wide at its widest point, and though most of the Americans there were tourists, we were not. We rented a house called The Moorings by the harbor. We settled in and made friends. My brother and I went to a school called Warwick Academy, where we helped drag brushwood to the top of a hill for a bonfire to celebrate the coronation of George the Sixth. All in all it seems to me, looking back, that I lived there with a greater sense of permanence than any place we had lived earlier where there had always been another job in the offing and another house to move to next. And with a sense of the magic and mystery of things greater than I had ever experienced this side of Oz.

There are those who say that William Shakespeare may have had Bermuda in mind when he wrote *The Tempest,* and that is perhaps part of why there are lines from that play that have haunted me all my life and speak better than anything else I know for the spell that island cast. It is a speech of Caliban's.

> Be not affeard, the Isle is full of noyses,
> Sounds, and sweet aires, that give delight and hurt not;
> Sometimes a thousand twangling Instruments
> Will hum about mine eares; and sometimes voices,
> That if I then had wak'd after long sleep,
> Will make me sleep again, and then in dreaming,
> The clouds methought would open and shew riches
> Ready to drop upon me, that when I wak'd
> I cried to dream again.

Be not affeard—maybe that was at the heart of it for me. With the worst having happened, there was no longer the worst to fear. Full fathom five my father lay, and part of the riches that dropped on me was the gift of forgetting him. We never really forget anything, they say, and all our pasts lie fathoms deep in us somewhere waiting for some stray sight or smell or scrap of sound to bring them to the surface again. But for the time at least, I let him go as completely as he had let go of us, and the space and peace of that were not the least of the gifts that the island gave.

And there were other gifts, too—sounds and sweet airs that gave delight and hurt not. Why I should have remembered it all these years, I can only guess, but one of them was a scene that can have lasted only a moment or two as I was wheeling my bicycle up a steep dirt lane. I have the impression of late afternoon sun and of dust in the air that the sun turned gold, of slowness and stillness and deepest privacy. I see shafts of sun aslant through palm leaves and the flaking plaster of a church rinsed in light back up the hill a way. Through the haze I see a priest come walking down toward me. He is dressed all in black with black gaiters and a low-crowned, broad-brimmed black hat like a priest out of Jane Austen or Laurence Sterne. I remember how out of place he looked, so dark and unyielding in all that unkempt greenness, and yet how much the place seemed somehow his. He passed me by without a word or a nod, he going his way, I going mine, and that was all. The golden air. The purposeful, dark figure passing by like a shadow or a foreshadowing. The sense of another time that I will carry with me to the end of my time.

I remember another much steeper hill that Jamie and I had to climb when we rode our bikes to the beach from school, and how when we got to the top of it, there, suddenly, was the unutterable, blinding blue-green flash of the ocean a mile or so away, and how in a single vast coast we would swoop down on it like birds. I remember a stout, hot-tempered Englishman named Mr. Sutton, who taught at Warwick Academy, and how he lit cigarettes with sun through a magnifying glass and called the two-by-four that he whacked you with if you misbehaved Sutton's pink pills for pale people. There were flat, sweet yellow buns that you could buy across the street. There were the kites that on Good Friday, for some reason, all the boys in the school went out in the fields to fly, and when you had coaxed your kite high enough, the whole great bellying length of string would start to hum like a thousand twangling instruments about your ears.

There were gifts like these—sights and sounds and smells that I had never known before, staggering in their newness, and there were also gifts I had been born with that the years in Bermuda gave me again in a way to make them seem new. Naya, for instance, came to stay with us for a while, the same old Naya I had served cold string beans to at the age of six, who had given me my taste for books and language and green salad and French, who for years had been teaching me my forebears like irregular verbs—the eccentric New England uncles and the miserly Swiss aunts who roistered through the Gilbert and Sullivan of her endless patter songs. She was the same, but I saw her new—saw her un-booked, un-Pittsburghed, as unhitched from her accustomed world as I was unhitched from mine so that we could meet again as if almost for the first time, like strangers taking shelter from the rain. She drank rum swizzles on the balcony at Twenty One. In flat-heeled shoes she walked coral roads by the mile. Down at the Furness Line docks once she accidentally set a heavy luggage cart rolling forward by sitting on it, and when my mother came to find us, what she found was Naya in her pearls and a beret held fast by a jet pin pitched like a stevedore to the task of helping my bare-legged brother and me wheel it back to where it belonged, and we laughed till the tears rolled down. I saw us ourselves for the first time as no less wondrously freakish than our freakish forebears had been, the creators of our own new legends.

And Grandma Buechner came too—like the Inspector General, we feared—came to run her white-gloved finger over the upper edges and lower sills of our lives, checking for unreality and extravagance, came to dust off a Scharmann maxim or two. I picture her stout figure looking down from the deck of the *Monarch* to see if she could spot us on the quay below to welcome her. I see her face—half Queen Victoria, half Gertrude Stein—with a sky full of gulls wheeling behind it. I hear her heavy, effortful tread in the hall of what was surely the only smoked salmon–colored house whose rent she ever paid. I had known her power all my life but had never before seen it pitted against an island. It was like trying to drive a breath of fresh air with a croquet mallet, like trying to plump the scent of mimosa into shape, and for as long as she was there, the island prevailed. She grew girlish and coy under the blandishments of the courtly men my mother presented to her. She breathed deep the cedar-laden, salt-sweet air and was as tipsy on it as the rest of us. But when she got home safe to New York again, she wrote my mother that letter about facing reality with the result that that fall we went back and faced it for a winter in an apartment on 90th Street between Lexington and Park. But when the winter was up, she condoned our going back because in the long run she loved us more even than she loved her principles, I suppose, and it was toward the end of that second and last year in Bermuda that I received what may have been the greatest of the gifts the island gave, without any clear idea what it was that I was receiving or that anybody had ever received the likes before.

She was a girl going on thirteen as I was, with a mouth

that turned up at the corners. If we ever spoke to each other about anything of consequence, I have long since forgotten it. I have forgotten the color of her eyes. I have forgotten the sound of her voice. But one day at dusk we were sitting side by side on a crumbling stone wall watching the Salt Kettle ferries come and go when, no less innocently than the time I reached up to the bust of Venus under my grandfather's raffish gaze, our bare knees happened to touch for a moment, and in that moment I was filled with such a sweet panic and anguish of longing for I had no idea what that I knew my life could never be complete until I found it. "Difference of sex no more we knew / Than our guardian angels do," as John Donne wrote, and in the ordinary sense of the word, no love could have been less erotic, but it was the Heavenly Eros in all its glory nonetheless—there is no question about that. It was the upward-reaching and fathomlessly hungering, heart-breaking love for the beauty of the world at its most beautiful, and, beyond that, for that beauty east of the sun and west of the moon which is past the reach of all but our most desperate desiring and is finally the beauty of Beauty itself, of Being itself and what lies at the heart of Being.

Like all children I had been brought up till then primarily on the receiving end of love. My parents loved me, my grandparents, a handful of others maybe, and I had accepted their love the way a child does, as part of the givenness of things, and responded to it the way a cat purrs when you pat it. But now for the first time I was myself the source and giver of a love so full to overflowing that I could not possibly have expressed it to that girl whose mouth turned up at the corners even if I had had the courage to try. And let anyone who dismisses such feelings as puppy love, silly love, be set straight because I suspect that rarely if ever again in our lives does Eros touch us in such a distilled and potent form as when we are children and have so little else in our hearts to dilute it. I loved her more than I knew how to say even to myself. Whether in any way she loved me in return, I neither knew nor, as far as I can remember, was even especially concerned to find out. Just to love her was all that I asked. Eros itself, even tinged with the sadness of knowing that I could never fully find on earth or sea whatever it was that I longed for, was gift enough.

Then, as unforeseeably as it had begun, it ended. On the first of September, Hitler's armies invaded Poland, and on the third, England and France declared war on Germany. The rumor soon spread that the Germans had plans to capture Bermuda for a submarine base, and all Americans were required to leave. It happened very suddenly, and in the haste and confusion of it, I never even knew when she left or had a chance to say goodbye. The *Monarch* and the *Queen* were painted gray for camouflage, and on the *Queen,* I think, with the portholes blacked out and no one allowed so much as to light a match on deck after dark, we set sail for a reality that we were forced, with the rest of the world, to face at last.

Whatever reality is. Reality is what is, I suppose, is whatever there is that seems real; and since what seems real to one need not seem real to another—like color to the blind, like hope to the hopeless—we all create our own realities as we go along. Reality for me was this. Out of my father's death there came, for me, a new and, in many ways, happier life. The shock of his death faded and so did those feelings about it which led me for a while to speak of it in terms of heart trouble because the word *suicide* seemed somehow shameful and better left unspoken. I cannot say the grief faded because, in a sense, I had not yet, unlike my brother, really felt that grief. That was not to happen for thirty years or more. But the grief was postponed, allowed to sink beneath the whole bright accumulation of the Bermuda years and many years that came later until only in my middle age did it become real enough for me to weep real tears over at last and to see better than I ever had earlier who it was that I was weeping for and who I was that was weeping. In that never-never land, that Oz of an island, where we had no roots, I found for the first time a sense of being rooted. In that land where as foreigners we could never really belong, I found a sense of belonging. In that most frivolous place that the travel brochures billed as the vacationers' paradise, I made what was perhaps the least frivolous discovery that I had made up till then, which was that love is not merely a warmth to bask in the way the boatloads of honeymooners basked in the warmth of Coral Beach but a grave, fierce yearning and reaching out for Paradise itself, a losing and finding of the self in the Paradise of another. This is the reality of those years as I look back at them, and part of their reality for me is that all the healing and strengthening that came my way then came my way largely as a gift and as a gift that implies a giver. Did it?

There are other ways of looking at those years, of course. The commonsense way would be to say simply that the boy grew up a little. Time heals all wounds, and his were no exception. Things started to fall in place for him, that's all. What happened happened as much by chance as the chance pattern of raindrops on a window-pane, as much by luck as happening to draw the lucky number in a raffle. If you want to speak in terms of a gift and a giver, then you should speak of the boy's grand-mother, that formidable old lady who seems to have gotten short shrift in this account, but who paid the rent after all and financed the whole operation even though it was against her better judgment to do so. Or there could be psychological ways. You could say that the trauma of the father's suicide was such that the boy, unable to come to terms with his own feelings, repressed them to the extent that they were bound to cause psycho-logical problems later on. You could speak in terms of Oedipal conflict and say that part of the reason the boy seemed to recover from his grief as quickly as he did was that, with his father's death, he got what, subconsciously, he had of course always wanted, which was his mother to himself. And you could say that one consequence of that might well have been just such a residue of anxiety and guilt as might in later years lead him to seek consola-tion in religious fantasy, to dream up for himself a father in Heaven to replace the one he had lost. As for the incident of the girl, it was clearly a case of adolescent sexuality romanticized to the level of a temporary obses-sion.

I cannot deny such ways of looking at those years, nor do I want to. These and many other such insights seem real to me. Yes, time heals all wounds or at least dresses them, makes them endurable. Yes, at the king's death, the grief of the prince is mitigated by becoming king himself. Yes, the great transfiguring power of sex stirs early and seismically in all of us. Which of us can look at our own religion or lack of it without seeing in it the elements of wish-fulfillment? Which of us can look back at our own lives without seeing in them the role of blind chance and dumb luck? But faith, says the author of the Epistle to the Hebrews, is "the assurance of things hoped for, the conviction of things not seen," and looking back at those distant years I choose not to deny, either, the compelling sense of an unseen giver and a series of hidden gifts as not only another part of their reality, but the deepest part of all.

My grandmother might have been right about our going to Bermuda. It could have been a terrible mistake. Instead maybe it was the best thing we ever did. My father's death could have closed doors in me once and for all against the possibility of ever giving entrance to such love and thereby to such pain again. Instead, it opened up some door in me to the pain of others—not that I did much about the others, God knows, or have ever done much about them since because I am too lily-livered for that, too weak of faith, too self-absorbed and squeamish —but such pain as I had known in my own life opened up, if not my hands to help much, at least my eyes to begin seeing anyway that there is pain in every life, even the apparently luckiest, that buried griefs and hurtful memories are part of us all. And there was so much else to see, too—the priest in his black gaiters, the pull and hum of the Good Friday kites, the girl sitting beside me on the wall at Salt Kettle—and there is so much to see always, things too big to take in all at once, things so small as hardly to be noticed. And though they may well come by accident, these moments of our seeing, I choose to believe that it is by no means by accident when they open our hearts as well as our eyes.

A crazy, holy grace I have called it. Crazy because whoever could have predicted it? Who can ever foresee the crazy how and when and where of a grace that wells up out of the lostness and pain of the world and of our own inner worlds? And holy because these moments of grace come ultimately from farther away than Oz and deeper down than doom, holy because they heal and hallow. "For all thy blessings, known and unknown, remembered and forgotten, we give thee thanks," runs an old prayer, and it is for the all but unknown ones and the more than half-forgotten ones that we do well to look back over the journeys of our lives because it is their presence that makes the life of each of us a sacred journey. We have a hard time seeing such blessed and blessing moments as the gifts I choose to believe they are and a harder time still reaching out toward the hope of a giving hand, but part of the gift is to be able, at least from time to time, to be assured and convinced without seeing, as Hebrews says, because that is of the very style and substance of faith as well as what drives it always to seek a farther and a deeper seeing still.

There will always be some who say that such faith is only a dream, and God knows there is none who can say it more devastatingly than we sometimes say it to ourselves, but if so, I think of it as like the dream that Caliban dreamed. Faith is like the dream in which the clouds open to show such riches ready to drop upon us that when we wake into the reality of nothing more than common sense, we cry to dream again because the

dreaming seems truer than the waking does to the fullness of reality not as we have seen it, to be sure, but as
by faith we trust it to be without seeing. Faith is both the
dreaming and the crying. Faith is the assurance that the
best and holiest dream is true after all. Faith in *something*
—if only in the proposition that life is better than death
—is what makes our journeys through time bearable.
When faith ends, the journey ends—ends either in a
death like my father's or in the living death of those who
believe themselves to be without hope.

For Adam and Eve, time started with their expulsion
from the garden. For me, it started with the opening of
a door. For all the sons and daughters of Eve, it starts at
whatever moment it is at which the unthinking and time-
less innocence of childhood ends, which may be either a
dramatic moment, as it was for me, or a moment or series
of moments so subtle and undramatic that we scarcely
recognize them. But one way or another the journey
through time starts for us all, and for all of us, too, that
journey is in at least one sense the same journey because
what it is primarily, I think, is a journey *in search*. Each
must say for himself what he searches for, and there will
be as many answers as there are searchers, but perhaps
there are certain general answers that will do for us all.
We search for a self to be. We search for other selves to
love. We search for work to do. And since even when to
one degree or another we find these things, we find also
that there is still something crucial missing which we
have not found, we search for that unfound thing too,
even though we do not know its name or where it is to
be found or even if it is to be found at all.

From Bermuda we moved to a small town in North Carolina called Tryon because Naya and Grandpa Kuhn had retired there from Pittsburgh and were living in a house in a valley ringed round by the Blue Ridge mountains where we went to live with them, pooling our resources with theirs. In neither case did those resources amount to very much—Grandpa Kuhn had for the second time in his life lost most of his money and we had nothing beyond our allowance from Grandma Buechner —and what I remember in many ways best of the year we lived there with them was a rich and faintly comic sense of *making do.* In Bermuda, it seemed to me, we had lived like kings; in Tryon we lived like kings in exile. We had our occasional sprees and extravagances—my brother and I went to a small private school run by Miss Hope Washburn, a short, wiry woman of great wryness and wit and erudition who said she looked like Savonarola and did; we had servants; we had a car—but there was always the feeling that unless we were careful, the cupboard some morning would be bare. And that, of course, only served to make what was in it seem all the more precious while it lasted.

Tryon in those days was a southern town full of elderly Yankees who had one way or another made their marks on the world, many of them, and had then retreated from it down there. Naya with her taste for the bizarre had a heyday. There was the retired Navy captain who piped ladies into his house with a bosun's whistle and his memorable wife who wore her honey-colored hair in pre-Raphaelite coils like Guinevere and had published a novel in London many years earlier, which was the closest that I had come by that point to what seemed to me true fame. There was a little woman with the head of a dwarf who would come to read Molière with Naya from time to time and another who in the midst of conversation would suddenly lower her eyes and raise her right hand as high as it would go above her head as if to fend off, or possibly welcome, some invisible intruder. There was a German baron who some said had been responsible for military atrocities in Belgium during the first world war and had a great record collection of Beethoven. And, as in Bermuda, there were the sounds and sweet airs—the sour smell of fat pine and dead leaves in the woods that surrounded our house, the dogwood and mountain laurel that blossomed in the spring, the redbud and forsythia. There were cardinals in the bird feeder, and the high blue hills. There were sweet grass baskets that the mountain people sold on Trade Street on Saturdays and a drugstore called Missildine's that smelled of medicine and newspapers and cologne and where they made strong, dark cokes at the soda fountain and grilled cheese sandwiches as heavy and limp as dead birds.

And there was a heavy, fat collection of colored reproductions of paintings called *A Treasury of Art Masterpieces,* edited by Thomas Craven, which at ten dollars a copy was the most expensive book I had ever owned and has been part of me ever since. Some of the faces are more vivid and alive for me now than the real faces of many of the people I knew and loved best then—Hogarth's *Shrimp Girl* especially, done all in warm sepia, umber, and rose with a platter of shrimp on her napkined head, and a mouth that turned up at the corners as she smiled, and under raised brows a pair of dark, shoe-button eyes with all of girlhood in them, so astonished and hopeful, so giddy and glad. And Albrecht Dürer's *Hieronymus Holzschuer,* overfed and choleric with his silvery hair spidered out on his brow, his silvery beard parted in the middle over the deep, soft sable collar of his robe. And Titian's *Man in a Red Cap,* the beautiful young Venetian with the neck and shoulders of a bull and a mystic's eyes. But of all of them, the one I remember best turns out not to be in Craven's book at all, but some other collection that must have come my way at the same time, and that is a pastel of the head of Jesus that Leonardo Da Vinci did as a study for *The Last Supper.* The head is tipped slightly to one side and down. He looks Jewish. He looks very tired. Some of the color has flaked away. His eyes are closed. That was the face that moved me and stayed with me more in a way than all the others, though not because it was Jesus' face, as far as I can remember, but just because it seemed the face of a human being to whom everything had happened that can happen. It was a face of great stillness, a face that had survived.

It was as if in the picture I caught a glimpse of someone whose presence I noted in a different way from the others. In the case of Hogarth's shrimp girl, for instance, what delighted me was the sense of seeing in her astonished young face a beauty that I had never seen anywhere else. In the case of Da Vinci's Jesus, on the other hand, what haunted me was so strong a feeling of the painter's having in some unimaginable way caught the likeness just right that it was as if, without knowing it, I had already seen deep within myself some vision of what he looked like or what I hoped he looked like on the basis of which I could affirm the picture's authenticity. I had come across many other representations of Jesus' face in my day, but this was one that I could somehow vouch for, and although I set it aside and gave no special thought to it, somewhere in the back of my mind I seem always to have kept track of it as though to have a way of recognizing him if ever our paths happened to cross again.

Naya and I went to the Episcopal church together from time to time. As a fairly free-wheeling Unitarian, Naya had never been a church-goer particularly, but it was something to do on a Sunday that did not cost much, a chance to see some of the Tryon eccentrics in another mode. One of them, a tall, red-haired man who was a skilled amateur chef and cocktail party luminary, was a soloist in the choir, and we used to love to hear him chant in his stately croak of a baritone, "O ye Sun and Moon, bless ye the Lord . . . . O ye Nights and Days, bless ye the Lord . . . . O ye Whales and all that moves in the waters, bless ye the Lord," and so on, with the rest of the choir quaveringly echoing each phrase with their "Praise him and magnify him forever." And I suppose in some way Naya and I praised and magnified him ourselves— praised and magnified something anyway: that though the world was at war, we were surviving, were making do. That there was love and lightness of heart enough from somewhere to keep our ship afloat, battered though it might be. And it was in that same church that my brother and I and a cousin of ours had ourselves chris- tened one odd day. Somehow we discovered that it had never been done before, and less from any religious motive, I think, than from simply a sense that like getting your inoculations and going to school, it was something you did, we went ahead and did it. Whether I associated the process in any way with that tired, Jewish face in the Da Vinci pastel, I no longer remember. But I rather doubt it.

Be that as it may, the result of all those paintings was that I decided I wanted to be a painter myself and especially a painter of faces. I copied faces out of Craven's book and tried doing them from life. I also made faces up out of my mind, and these were apt to be very old and wrinkled like some I had seen in Rembrandt, except for one fatter, less ancient face which I kept drawing again and again and which could have been King Rinkitink or the Emperor Claudius or Mr. Pickwick or Louis the Sixteenth as the actor Robert Morley wonderfully portrayed him in a movie called *Marie Antoinette* that came out about then and took its place in my imagination beside those other sagas of men who, despite their apparent helplessness and foolishness, are the stuff of which true heroes are made.

It was the face, the surface, that interested me then at the age of thirteen, and I have wondered since how much this may have been Naya's influence because for her too it was the outward and visible oddities of people that she delighted in and was so good at caricaturing. And I have wondered, too, if for both of us this was a way of steering clear of the inward invisibleness beneath the face because there was so much more down there than either of us could well cope with, she because she was too old, I suppose, and I because I was too young.

Tryon, like Bermuda before it, was an in-between time, a time between childhood and whatever it is that takes childhood's place, a time when much was stirring beneath the surface but the surface itself remained in most ways unchanged, and therefore I tended to cling to it like a raft in a storm. Wherever we lived, home was still basically my family—the people I knew best, the faces I had known always. Home was the givenness of things, and the self I was was pretty much of a givenness, too. I was the name I had been given—Freddy, to distinguish me from Fred, who was my father. I was the oldest one, the one my mother and brother looked to. I was the bookish one, the one who loved rain, the one who could listen endlessly to Naya's endless and, to me, endlessly fascinating tales, the one who had inherited her taste for words and was destined to succeed her as the repository of the family past, or at least as much of it as could be contained in anecdotes which by definition avoided anything like the depth and darkness of the past except on the rare occasions when I pressed to know more. She avoided depth like the plague, the old escape artist, and already predisposed to do the same myself, I only too gladly followed her. I was the one who was not what I felt Grandma Buechner would have preferred me to be —which was my father's son as well as, if not instead of, my mother's: a boy who loved football and the out-of-doors as my father had loved them, a strong swimmer, a good dancer, a boy who could make his own way more and had more to say for himself and was tougher as the Scharmanns were tough. I knew in my heart that she was probably right, and the sadness of knowing that was another part of the self I was given.

So this time in my life was an in-between time in the sense, too, that I lived in between, was hedged in by, the people I loved who were all telling me who I was in a way that I could hardly help but give ear to since the other voices that were telling me who I was, the voices that spoke to me out of the world beyond the world of home, were by comparison such faint and ambiguous voices. There was the voice of falling in love with the girl in Bermuda, for instance, and of all the beauty I longed for beyond the beauty I longed for in her. There was the voice of mystery and magic as I had heard it not only in books, but had caught echoes of in the firefly dusks of earliest childhood, the priest in the lane, the extraordinary paintings of faces, and especially the painting of that one extraordinary face. And beyond the voices of home, there was also the voice of my own adolescent longing and loneliness, confusion and terror, which whispered to me that such inner realities were not always something you ignored the way everybody at home seemed to ignore them, but something that in the long run you had to face up to, like the old woman in Grandma Buechner's joke, even at the risk of losing one eye. I needed somebody other than those closest to me to share my own innerness with. I needed a home away from home, as the saying goes, needed a self of my own to be at home in. And the one who had most to lose by my breaking loose to find those things was the same one who did most to help me break loose because after that year in Tryon it was my mother who decided that it was time for me to go away to school, even though she was as dependent on me in her way as I was dependent on her in mine. It was one of her greatest gifts to me.

Lawrenceville was the name of the school in New Jersey that I went to that fall before Pearl Harbor, and pimply, nonathletic, my mother's son, I sat under the maples by the tennis courts with my tears staining the paper and wrote what I hoped were cheerful letters home. I pictured the terrace under the sleeping porch where I had loved to lie reading in a ragged canvas hammock, pictured Grandpa Kuhn sitting in the living room with his straw hat on listening to the war news on the radio, pictured my brother and a cousin trying to make a mud dam across the muddy little Pacolet river. But my homesickness was not just a longing for home, I think. It was a fear that home would somehow get lost before I ever got a chance to see it again, or that I would somehow get lost myself, and as things turned out, my fears proved well grounded on both points. That fall my mother was married to a widower she had known in Bermuda so that home was no longer North Carolina but New England, and before the end of that first year away at school, I was no longer the boy who had sat under the maples in tears.

It is hard to evoke the year 1940 for people who were not alive then—the great excitement of it, the extraordinary sense of aliveness. It was the war that did it, of course. I doubt if there has ever been a war that seemed so much a struggle between the forces of light and the forces of darkness because, although Hitler, Mussolini, Tojo, have come to seem since no worse than crazy uncles at a wake—criminals and lunatics, to be sure, but part of the human family at least, part of the same history that produces us all—at the time they seemed the very incarnation and caricature of evil. In America, on the other hand, we had for a leader that same president whom I had seen in the Mayflower, held upright under the arms by his two sons, but a pillar of strength and stability now who had been president for so long that he seemed to embody the very continuity of civilization that the war imperiled. For people born since, it must be hard to imagine a time when this country seemed so much on the side of the angels or a cause so just. Even as a child I had sensed the purposelessness and disillusion of the Depression years—I remember the anti-Roosevelt jokes, the anti-W.P.A. jokes, the roads into Washington when we lived there jammed by the jalopies of the gaunt, unshaven Hunger Marchers, remembered my own father's years of rootless wandering—and all of this was suddenly gone now with rich and poor alike caught up in a sense of common purpose and destiny. Ingenuous, sentimental, propagandizing as they were, you could not watch the great war movies like *Mrs. Miniver* and *In Which We Serve* unmoved, and when the theater lights came on at the end and "The Star Spangled Banner" was piped out over the loudspeaker system, you stood to it stirred in ways that in this post-Hiroshima, post-Dallas, post-Vietnam, post-Watergate age is perhaps no longer possible and may never be possible again. The war tapped reserves of strength and emotion that for years had gone forgotten or unrecognized, and this was true not only for the nation as a whole, but for the little nation of the school where I went and in some measure for me as a part of it.

The art class that I was assigned to was taught by a man who was an excellent draughtsman. He painted marvelous still lifes of almost photographic clarity—translucent glass vases of roses, bowls of sunlit fruit—and in order to teach us to do the same, he set us to making charcoal sketches of spheres, cubes, pyramids with the object of showing us how by getting the perspective right and the proper play of light and shade we could create the illusion of depth. All of this was fine for people who wanted to do still lifes, I thought, but it was not fine for me. It was not still life that interested me but alive life. Most particularly it was the endless and subtly changing variations of the human face—the moist glitter of eyes, the shadow of lips, the way the hair grew—and it was not long before I decided that if I could not paint what I wanted, then I did not want to be a painter at all.

At the same time I happened to have for an English teacher an entirely different sort of man. He had nothing of the draughtsman about him, no inclination to drill us in anything, but instead a tremendous, Irishman's zest for the blarney and wizardry of words. I had always been a reader and loved words for the tales they can tell and the knowledge they can impart and the worlds they can conjure up like the Scarecrow's Oz and Claudius' Rome; but this teacher, Mr. Martin, was the first to give me a feeling for what words are, and can do, in themselves. Through him I started to sense that words not only convey something, but *are* something; that words have color, depth, texture of their own, and the power to evoke vastly more than they mean; that words can be used not merely to make things clear, make things vivid, make things interesting and whatever else, but to make things happen inside the one who reads them or hears them. When Gerard Manley Hopkins writes a poem about a blacksmith and addresses him as one who "didst fettle for the great gray drayhorse his bright and battering sandal," he is not merely bringing the blacksmith to life, but in a way is bringing us to life as well. Through the sound, rhythm, passion of his words, he is bringing to life in us, as might otherwise never have been brought to life at all, a sense of the uniqueness and mystery and holiness not just of the blacksmith and his great gray drayhorse, but of reality itself, including the reality of ourselves. Mr. Martin had us read wonderful things—it was he who gave me my love for *The Tempest,* for instance—but it was a course less in literature than in language and the great power that language has to move and in some measure even to transform the human heart.

He had us do a good deal of writing, of course, and one day I got a paper back from him with what in an English class was the unheard-of grade of 100. It was an extremely overripe character sketch of an eighteenth century French courtier, like the ones I had seen in the *Marie Antoinette* movie, pulling on a pair of jeweled gloves as he stands on a balcony watching the sun go down, but it was as full of as many rich and marvelous words as I could dig up, and when he gave me 100 on it, I think it is not too much to say that, from that moment on, I knew that what I wanted to be more than anything else was a writer.

What I wanted to write especially was poetry, and I have wondered since why. The answer, I suspect, is that after all those childhood years of wandering around the surface of the east coast, after all the different places I had lived and schools I had been to, after all the tales Naya had told me of still other places, other people, I had had enough of breadth for a while, enough of surface, enough even of faces. What I was suddenly most drawn to now was the dimension of what lay beneath the surface and behind the face. What was going on inside myself, behind my own face, was the subject I started trying to turn to in my half-baked way, and I suppose it was no coincidence that, for the first time in my life, I began to be able to tell a few friends the true story of how my father had died, which was the innermost secret I had.

Chief among these friends was my friend Jimmy Merrill, who had a "cube" across the corridor from mine—cubes being the cheerless little three-sided cells where they housed the younger boys in those days with only a curtain at the open side for privacy. Like me, he was either no good at sports and consequently disliked them, or possibly the other way around. Like me—though through divorce rather than death—he had lost his father. Like me, he was a kind of oddball—plump and not very tall then with braces on his teeth and glasses that kept slipping down the short bridge of his nose and a rather sarcastic, sophisticated way of speaking that tended to put people off—and for that reason, as well as for the reason that he was a good deal brighter than most of us, including me, boys tended to make his life miserable. But it was Jimmy who became my first great friend, and it was through coming to know him that I discovered that perhaps I was not, as I had always suspected, alone in the universe and the only one of my kind. He was another who saw the world enough as I saw it to make me believe that maybe it was the way the world actually was—who cried at the same kinds of things that made me cry, and laughed at the same kind of foolery, and was helpless, hapless, ludicrous in many of the ways I felt I was. The Jigger Shop was the place that the whole school flocked to for candy and food and college banners and athletic equipment and Heaven only knows what-all else, and I remember being there one crowded Saturday afternoon when, in an excess of high spirits, another boy I knew dashed a dollop of tomato ketchup in my face from the bottle he was anointing his hamburger with, where-upon Jimmy handed me a great spoonful of butterscotch sauce from the sundae he had just ordered, and I smeared it lavishly down first one of my assailant's red cheeks and then the other with spectacular effect. Singly we could neither of us ever have pulled it off. Together we were a match for the world.

And together, too, we wrote poetry. We were end-lessly impressed by each other's work, but we were also the keenest rivals, and in poem after poem competed for prizes and grades and the marvel of our teachers. As I look back over the ones that I wrote, I cringe with embar-rassment at their terrible staginess and bathos, but I can remember still the enormous excitement of writing them, of waking up in the morning and looking at the poem of the evening before with the richest possible sense of having written something that seemed to me beautiful, lasting, and true. What I cannot remember is what it was that led me in so many of them to make references to Jesus. I had forgotten that I had until I looked back at them recently. It is true that I joined a confirmation class at school, of which I remember abso-lutely nothing except the dark, thin-boned profile of the young Episcopal priest who taught it and the fact that I was eventually confirmed in the school chapel by the florid, medieval-looking Bishop of New Jersey. But I have the feeling that I gave no more serious thought to what I was doing than when I had arranged for my own christening a year or so earlier. If I had to guess at my motive for putting Jesus in so many of my poems, I would guess that it was for effect as much as anything, to give them some sort of aura or authority that I was afraid they lacked, to suggest that I was a much more substantial and fancier poet than I secretly believed myself to be. Maybe, too, I remembered the Da Vinci study for *The Last Supper* and hoped that the mention of his name might touch people as much as the sight of that sad, tired face had touched me. I do not know. But for whatever the reason or lack of one, I find to my surprise that Jesus appears again and again in those early, embarrassing poems as he has appeared in many another embarrassing poem both before and since. I cannot explain why he is there any more than I can explain why he is anywhere. And perhaps the explanation is not important. He was there, of all places, even there, and that is important enough.

We search, on our journeys, for a self to be, for other selves to love, and for work to do, and by the June I graduated from Lawrenceville, just a month short of seventeen, I had come farther along the way to discovering at least something of each than I believe I supposed at the time.

It is all but impossible, I think, to remember, in any very inward sense, any of the selves that we have been along the way, to recapture, from the vantage of thirty, forty, fifty, what it felt like to be sixteen. But I can remember at least the sense of having become, or started to become, a self with boundaries somewhat wider than and different from those set me by my family. I no more knew who I was then than in most ways I know who I am now, but I knew that I could survive more or less on my own in more or less the real world. I knew, as I had not before, the sound of my own voice both literally and figuratively—knew something of what was different about my way of speaking from anybody else's way and knew something of the power of words spoken from the truth of my own heart or from as close to that truth as I was able to come then. In Tryon, with the onset of adolescence and knocked silly by all the dreams, hungers, fears that I figured I was going to have to live with for the rest of my days, I remember my scalp going cold at the thought that nothing was real, least of all me. There were nightmarish times when even those closest to me seemed strangers as I seemed a stranger to myself, and I was sure that I must be losing my mind. But by sixteen I had found others, both like me and unlike me, and if they could be my friends, I decided, then I must be real enough and sane enough at least to get by.

And I loved them, these others, those friends and teachers. I would never have used the word *love,* saving that for what I had felt for the girl with the mouth that turned up at the corners, and for Naya, my mother and brother, but love of a kind it nonetheless was. Even the ones I did not all that much like I think I knew I would miss when the time came. I sensed in them, as in myself, an inner battle against loneliness and the great dark, and to know that they were also battling was to be no longer alone in the same way within myself. I loved them for that. I wished them well. And then there was Jimmy, my first fast friend; and Huyler, who of all of them heard out most healingly the secret of my father; and Bill, skinny and full of life and the brightest of us all, who would have added God only knows what richness to the great ragbag of things if the war had not ended him before he more than got started. I could not imagine who I would have been without them, nor can I imagine it to this day because they are in so many ways a part of me still.

And if part of my search, those Lawrenceville years, was the search also for a father, I found fathers galore—Mr. Martin, who may have just changed the whole course of my life with that one preposterous grade; and Mr. Thurber, who gave hour after hour to going over with me in great detail those ghastly, promising poems; and Mr. Bowman, my Greek teacher, who was mad as a hatter and recommended that I read Norman Douglas' *South Wind* because he said it would corrupt me; and Mr. Heely, the headmaster, who on the day before school was to start once said to his faculty, "Gentlemen, never forget that when you enter your classrooms tomorrow, you will frequently find yourselves in the presence of your intellectual superiors." On All Saints' Day, it is not just the saints of the church that we should remember in our prayers, but all the foolish ones and wise ones, the shy ones and overbearing ones, the broken ones and whole ones, the despots and tosspots and crackpots of our lives who, one way or another, have been our particular fathers and mothers and saints, and whom we loved without knowing we loved them and by whom we were helped to whatever little we may have, or ever hope to have, of some kind of seedy sainthood of our own.

And I found work to do. By the time I was sixteen, I knew as surely as I knew anything that the work I wanted to spend my life doing was the work of words. I did not yet know what I wanted to say with them. I did not yet know in what form I wanted to say it or to what purpose. But if a vocation is as much the work that chooses you as the work you choose, then I knew from that time on that my vocation was, for better or worse, to involve that searching for, and treasuring, and telling of secrets which is what the real business of words is all about.

Something like all of this was what I had at least started to find by the spring of 1943 with the world at war and in a way more alive to the issues of light and dark than it has ever been since. What I had not found, I could not name and, for the most part, knew of only through my sense of its precious and puzzling and haunting absence. And maybe we can never name it by its final, true, and holy name, and maybe it is largely through its absence that, this side of Paradise, we will ever know it.

III

Beyond Time

THE CROW of a rooster. Two carpenters talking at their work in another room. The tick-tock of a clock on the wall. The rumble of your own stomach. Each sound can be thought of as meaning something, if it is meaning you want. After some years now of living with roosters, I know that their crow does not mean that the sun is coming up because they crow off and on all day long with their silly, fierce heads thrown back and the barnyard breeze in their tail feathers. Maybe it means that they are remembering the last time it came up or thinking ahead to the next time. Maybe it means only that they are roosters being roosters. The voices and hammering in the other room mean that not everybody in the world sits around mooning over the past, but that the real business of life goes on and somewhere the job is getting done; means, too, that life is a mystery. What are they talking about? What are they making? The ticking of the clock is death's patter song and means that time passes and passes and passes, whatever time is. The rumbling stomach means hunger and lunch. But meaning in that sense is not the point, or at least not my point. My point is that all those sounds together, or others like them, are the sound of our lives.

What each of them might be thought to mean separately is less important than what they all mean together. At the very least they mean this: mean *listen*. Listen. Your life is happening. You are happening. You, the rooster, the clock, the workmen, your stomach, are all happening together. A journey, years long, has brought each of you through thick and thin to this moment in time as mine has also brought me. Think back on that journey. Listen back to the sounds and sweet airs of your journey that give delight and hurt not and to those too that give no delight at all and hurt like Hell. *Be not affeard.* The music of your life is subtle and elusive and like no other—not a song with words but a song without words, a singing, clattering music to gladden the heart or turn the heart to stone, to haunt you perhaps with echoes of a vaster, farther music of which it is part.

The question is not whether the things that happen to you are chance things or God's things because, of course, they are both at once. There is no chance thing through which God cannot speak—even the walk from the house to the garage that you have walked ten thousand times before, even the moments when you cannot believe there is a God who speaks at all anywhere. He speaks, I believe, and the words he speaks are incarnate in the flesh and blood of our selves and of our own footsore and sacred journeys. We cannot live our lives constantly looking back, listening back, lest we be turned to pillars of longing and regret, but to live without listening at all is to live deaf to the fullness of the music. Sometimes we avoid listening for fear of what we may hear, sometimes for fear that we may hear nothing at all but the empty rattle of our own feet on the pavement. But *be not affeard,* says Caliban, nor is he the only one to say it. "Be not afraid," says another, "for lo, I am with you always, even unto the end of the world." He says he is with us on our journeys. He says he has been with us since each of our journeys began. Listen for him. Listen to the sweet and bitter airs of your present and your past for the sound of him.

When I listen to the sounds of college all those years ago, I hear the clatter of feet on stone steps and wooden steps, the rifle-shot slap of books dropped to the writing arms of seats in lecture halls, the calling of voices through the autumn dark of Holder court three stories below my room, and the playing of everybody's phonograph at once—"Honeysuckle Rose," "People Will Say We're in Love," "As Time Goes By." Late one night the Princeton gym catches fire and the whole campus tumbles out of bed, bars, parties to watch as the twin Gothic turrets at the main entrance shoot flames up to twice the height of the turrets themselves with courtly old Dean Radcliffe Heermance standing there in his bathrobe and slippers, and the proctors and campus cops, the boozing, sleep-eyed, milling undergraduates singing their songs—"Keep the Home Fires Burning," "Over There"—their faces on fire with the towering flames. And over there, London is also on fire, and they say that Hyde Park is carpeted with crocuses purple as flame, and botanists haunt bomb craters for flowers, unknown since the great fire of 1666, brought to life by nitrates from the burning bombs, life blossoming out of death, beauty out of pain, the past out of the present, these fundamental things of life as time goes by.

In the Nassau Tavern, the only black man in a crowd of chug-a-lugging white boys makes his way to the bar where he orders a beer. Without either a word or any need for one, the bartender slaps it down on the counter and watches it being drunk till the glass is empty, then takes the glass from the black man's hand and dashes it to pieces on the stone floor.

Albert Einstein lives with his daughter in a little house on Mercer Street, and I often see him walking to town in his button-up sweater that looks knitted with saplings, his great head of hair in a tangle, and his sad, spaniel eyes brimming with secrets. He does a little girl's arithmetic for her, they say, and she pays him with gumdrops. I see him buy records in the music store, hear the sudden hush as he enters McCosh 10 packed to the rafters to hear Bertrand Russell lecture on the laws of chance. In a couple of years, two Japanese cities vanish from the face of the earth without a chance, and one of his secrets is out of the bag at last.

It is one farewell party after another as friends enlist or get drafted, a series of wild, drunken jokes that old Bill, old Peter, old somebody, is going off to do his sad-sack best half cock-eyed on bourbon or beer or rum-and-coke; but at the heart of every sad-sack joke there is sadness. Not even the parties can drown it out altogether. Not even work can, and nobody works much anyway because it's here today and gone tomorrow, gone, and what is the point.

I took German like medicine, hoping that it might land me in Intelligence when my time came instead of the Infantry, and almost flunked it despite artful cribbing from Rainer Maria Rilke in my German compositions. I took medieval history, I no longer remember why, and out of it all, the one thing that stuck by me was Saint Francis of Assisi and his Canticle to the Sun. *"Laudato sie, misigniore,"* he sang—praise to thee, *misigniore,* for Brother Sun, for Sister Moon, and though there was much in it that reminded me of the creaking baritone in the Tryon church where I sometimes went with Naya, there was a passion to it that was new to me and a mystery too because it was not just Brother Sun and Sister Moon that he was giving praise for in his canticle but Sister Death too, of all things, death no less than life as sister and friend. I had heard before of praising God, but the madness of Saint Francis' praise was new to me, the madness of throwing away everything he ever had or ever hoped to have for love of the creation no less than of the creator, of making a marvelous and holy fool of himself by tramping out into the fields to tell swallows and sky-larks and red-winged blackbirds that they ought to praise God too for the air that bore them up and for their nests in the high trees.

I took creative writing, too—wondering, as I still do, what other kind of writing there is—and wrote poems about Saint Francis, about flying kites in Bermuda on Good Friday, about war and love, but in all of them I think my chief interest was less in trying to tell some kind of truth, if only a truth about myself or what I had seen, than in trying to make an effect. "You have a way with words," my instructor, the critic R. P. Blackmur, told me, and although at the time it was like getting the Pulitzer Prize, it seems to me now that there was also a barb to his remark. I wrote poems with punch lines, had a way of making words ring out and dance a little, but there was little if any of my life's blood in my poems. I was writing for my teachers, for glory. I had not yet started trying to write either out of myself very much or for myself, partly, of course, because I had only a very dim sense of who that self was, and what with both the war and my eighteenth birthday bearing down on me hard, there was precious little time to find out. We had the sense—all of us, I think—that our time was running out, and that was why we tried to fill it as full as we did with whatever came to hand, why in the face of death it was a time with so much life in it. There was so much to do, so much to be, so much to read. John Donne I read especially, and William Blake, and T. S. Eliot, more carried away with the sound of their voices than with what they said—the stammering intensity of Donne, the toying, crazy innocence of Blake, and Eliot so weary and civilized and under control, the wisest old possum of them all.

And there were weekends in New York, during which I often thought how in five hundred or a thousand years, if the world should last that long, archeologists would give their right arms for just one glimpse of what I was seeing for free—all the life and color and movement of that great city exactly as it was in the forties of the twentieth century A.D. Penn Station swarming with uniforms and terrible good-byes. Broadway blacked out. Young ensigns up from Naval ROTC and girls down from Vassar and Smith, meeting under the Biltmore's ineffable clock as though they had all the time in the world. And the endless parties to get drunk at, the cigarettes to smoke before anybody much decided they were bad for you, the famous books to buy, though you knew perfectly well you would never read them but just for the honor of having them on your shelf, the excitement of bouncing your first check, the old friends from Lawrenceville and the new friends from everywhere else, all of them caught up with you in the swift and tumbling torrent of it.

But no matter how swiftly the torrent tumbles, there come moments when, rounding a bend or where the streambed deepens, it flattens out suddenly to a surface so slow and smooth that you can almost see down to the bottom of it. I had run into debt. I waited on tables in freshman commons to help eke out my scholarship, but I hated the job, felt demeaned by it, and skipped so many meals that I ended up making less in wages than I owed in fines. A hundred dollars was all I needed to see me through, but in those days that seemed like a thousand. So I wrote to the younger of my father's two younger brothers asking if I could come see him at his New York office but not mentioning why for fear he might turn me down before I got the chance to make my pitch in person. He was the intellectual of my father's family, a little on the brash side, very successful in the advertising business despite or because of the fact that he thought it a preposterous business to be in, especially with the war going on, and of all of them, he was the one who, I was always told, had been the most critical of my father for doing what he had done. He had always been very kind to me, but I took my debt to him half paralyzed with guilt and apprehension only to hear him laugh when I finally stammered it out and say that of course I should have come and of course he would help. He wrote me out a check for my hundred dollars without so much as a murmur of reproof and walked me to the elevator, and I still remember the sight of him standing there in the shiny corridor, so trim and fit and resourceful as the elevator doors slid shut between us. It was not more than two or three weeks later that while I was away at a dance at a girl's school in Connecticut I got a telegram signed with his name asking me to call. When somebody answered the phone, I asked to speak to my uncle, and there was a clumsy silence at the other end of the line. Then his son and namesake, my cousin and childhood friend, came on and told me that early that morning, before anybody was up, his father had walked out of his bedroom into the next room and shot himself.

When the river slows down at a bend or deepens, currents from below wrinkle the silken surface and, if a leaf drifts by, catch it and spin it around and around and around; and if the current is strong enough, the leaf is sucked under, or if the leaf is lucky enough, it spins free and continues downstream into the swift white water beyond. It was the sheer melodrama of it that spun me around first—one brother, then another brother, like a family curse to be handed down from one generation to the next till some ancient, unknown wrong was righted at last. It was too bad to be true, too outlandish to grieve over properly any more than you can grieve over *The Fall of the House of Usher.* Even my cousin's voice on the phone seemed to have less of grief in it than of astonishment. And in her chair by the window, my Grandmother

Buechner received the news that could have been the end of her, and it was not the end.

When it got into the newspapers, I felt myself expected to play some sort of tragic role that in a way I had no true heart for. What might have sucked me under was not the grief but the fear of it—the fear that there might really be some fatal family flaw that I had inherited like the cut of my jaw or that, by some grim process of auto-suggestion if nothing else, I would end up as those two brothers had. The fear was real enough to make me for the first time in my life seek out a minister for help, partly because I really needed help and partly because I felt that I was expected to need it and had just enough taste for the dramatic to savor a little playing at least that much of the part. He was no help at all, as it turned out—a handsome, cheerful, piano-playing man who was obviously uncomfortable with what I had come to tell him and eager to talk about almost anything else. So we sat on his lawn in the sun and talked about this and that, and maybe that was part of the help I needed. In any case, I spun free of the dark eddy. I was lucky, in other words, and more than anything, I think, my luck was my worldly loving of the world and of my life in it too much to be able to imagine ever seriously wanting to abandon them. I loved the riches ready to drop upon me, loved the *laudato sie, misigniore* of things, and the pure thingness of things too, of people and parties and books to read and poems to write and places to go and risks to run and beauty to love. Brother Sun and Sister Moon—they seemed more than a match for the darkness of things; and it was by grace of nothing more if nothing less than sheer earthly delight in the gift to me of the earth and of my own life under the sun and moon that I was carried past the dangerous, downward pull of my uncle's death.

The next winter I sat in Army fatigues somewhere near Anniston, Alabama, eating my supper out of a mess kit. The infantry training battalion that I had been assigned to was on bivouac. There was a cold drizzle of rain, and everything was mud. The sun had gone down. I was still hungry when I finished and noticed that a man nearby had something left over that he was not going to eat. It was a turnip, and when I asked him if I could have it, he tossed it over to me. I missed the catch, the turnip fell to the ground, but I wanted it so badly that I picked it up and started eating it anyway, mud and all. And then, as I ate it, time deepened and slowed down again. With a lurch of the heart that is real to me still, I saw suddenly, almost as if from beyond time altogether, that not only was the turnip good, but the mud was good too, even the drizzle and cold were good, even the Army that I had dreaded for months. Sitting there in the Alabama winter with my mouth full of cold turnip and mud, I could see at least for a moment how if you ever took truly to heart the ultimate goodness and joy of things, even at their bleakest, the need to praise someone or something for it would be so great that you might even have to go out and speak of it to the birds of the air.

And for the first time I discovered that the earth as earth was also good. I had never known much of the earth before. It had never been the wildness and wetness of things that I had loved as much as shelter from wildness and wetness. I had loved roofs and umbrellas and home and the haven of books. Both literally and figuratively I had been mainly an indoors person up till then, and part of the pleasure for me of walls lined with books was that they made the walls stouter still to keep the out-of-doors out. What two years in the Army gave me more than anything else, I think, was a stronger sense than I had had since the firefly chases and beaches and Bermudas of childhood, of the earth itself as in some sense haven and home too. We crawled on our bellies over the shaggy hide of it with live machine gun fire crackling over our tails. We dug foxholes in it and crouched in them for hours on the rifle range. We marched on it, thirty miles at a throw, and learned how to puzzle our way across it with compass and maps. We slept on it in tents. I remember coming back from the infiltration course once so covered with mud that we were ordered into the cold showers with all our clothes still on our backs and our mud-caked rifles still in our hands, and there peeled off the layers one by one until we were ready to sprint back to the barracks naked as birth through the wet snow and a cold so intense that the mind almost cracked like ice. I remember the warmth of coal stoves and sunlight, the comfort of hot water, when you could find any, and of plain, honest food that stuck to your ribs. If I was not yet ready to praise God for it all, I praised my lucky stars anyway for the simple reason that the praise rose up in me as fierce and unbidden as tears. I had no choice.

The climax of infantry training then was the attack and capture of a simulated German village. With steel helmets and bayonets fixed, we fanned out through the make-believe streets and scarred wooden houses firing ammunition that was not make-believe and throwing live grenades through open windows. At some point, a short, stocky second lieutenant not much older than I was ordered me to climb up on a roof for some reason. I must have been perfectly capable of doing it physically after all those weeks of training, but all of a sudden I knew that I was not capable of it humanly. My body refused to work. My will refused to work. The lieutenant shouted himself the color of brick, and I suppose if it had been a real battle, I could have done it because my life would have depended on it; but as things were, it was as if something more than just my life depended on not doing it. Everything I was, everything I had ever hoped to be, everything I held precious and important and good somehow hung in the balance. Then something broke inside me, and I remember hearing the sounds I made as if somebody else was making them, the sounds of someone struggling for breath, for life. So they led me off and sat me down under a tree where the company commander came and talked to me with unexpected kindness, and I told him about my father, of all things, as though that somehow explained everything, which maybe in some sense it did. The result of it was that I was disqualified for combat duty, and though I would be proud to be able to report that the patriot in me was filled with disappointment, the truth of it is that I felt nothing so much as unspeakable relief. I was certain that my life had been saved by what had happened, and though what had happened was by no means an act I consciously put on in order to save it, a dim sense that that would probably be the result of it may well have been at least part of what paralyzed me. However that may be, it would have been entirely characteristic of who I was then. No one could have been more self-centered than I was at eighteen, and I doubt if any cause or any person can have seemed as important to me as my own survival.

I was just a week short of twenty when I was finally discharged after months of compiling AWOL and VD reports and other somewhat less than vital statistics, and once again I missed my chance to be a hero. We were lined up in alphabetical order, ready to march into the Army chapel where the discharge ceremony was to take place, when I was called aside by the officer in charge. I might have noticed, he explained in an undertone, that the man at the head of the line was black, and would I mind, therefore, taking my place in front of him as unobtrusively as possible so that the ceremony could proceed with proper decorum. Accustomed as we all of us were in those days to accepting such things as simply the way the world worked, I probably did not even consider protesting any more than I had protested the behavior of the bartender at the Nassau Tavern. But even if I had considered it, I doubt I would have protested for fear that it might somehow endanger my own getting out of the Army then and there. So I went and stood where I had been told and within moments stepped out of the chapel as free a man as it is possible to be in a country where not everybody is free. But the memory has haunted me ever since and with it the thought of the pathetic but who knows how telling a little blow I might have struck for common decency. "My own heart let me more have pity on," Gerard Manley Hopkins wrote, "let / Me live to my own sad self hereafter kind, / Charitable . . . Soul, self; come, poor Jackself, I do advise / You, jaded, let be; call off thoughts a while / Elsewhere." But it is not always an easy matter to call them off.

Concern for myself was the hallmark of those years, I am afraid, and one of the less embarrassing poems I wrote at Princeton speaks of it more clearly than I believe I was aware at the time.

> I drew a circle once around me there
> And set it spinning slowly through the air;
> I searched the disc of silence that it spanned
> To find some thing that I could understand.
> There was a tree
> Who bowed her head to me
> And folded in her roots a pool of rain
> Wherein she bowed again.
> There was a cloud, a sun; in fact somewhere
> I think that God was there
> And, as far as I could see, all mystery.
> Loving, living and alone
> I stood as silent as a stone
> Until within the center of my ring
> I found myself, and that was everything.

I have no idea what I would have said that I had found in finding myself if anybody had asked me, but I suspect that it was not a discovery of any great depth. I had given very little thought to the kind of person I was or to what there had been about my life to make me that way. I do not think that it occurred to me then to wonder much about the kind of person I was becoming or not becoming. I knew that I wanted to be a writer, but I had no clear idea what I wanted to write about; and as to the question of why I wanted to be a writer, I believe that, apart from simply the great fun of it for me, it was as much as anything to become famous enough not to have to explain to strangers how to pronounce my difficult last name. To be famous, it seemed to me, would be no longer to have to worry about explaining who I was even to myself because what fame meant was to be so known that in a sense I would no longer be a stranger to anybody.

What I think may actually have been true in my line about finding myself was not that I had found out anything very significant about who I was, but that I had found out something about what I could do. I knew that, as R. P. Blackmur had said, I had a way with words. When I spoke, no less than when I wrote, I had a way of making people listen. Both at Lawrenceville and in the Army, I had had some success as an actor. I knew that with words I could make at least some kind of bridge across the vast distance that separates the inner solitude of each of us from the inner solitude of everybody else. I knew that through no greater effort than that I could make good friends easily. And I knew I was lucky. "You always float to the surface," was the way Blackmur put it in another of his oracular utterances once, and it seemed to me that at least the recent facts bore him out. What with almost flunking German as a freshman and doing such a miserable job as a waiter, I came close to losing my scholarship, but in the end I did not lose it. When I got into debt, Uncle Tom came to the rescue, and later on in my college years, money always seemed to turn up from somewhere when I needed it. "Freddy is like royalty," a friend of mine once said. "He never pays." And of course I had also come through the war relatively unscathed when many a braver and better had not come through it at all.

"Within the center of my ring / I found myself, and that was everything," the poem says. Whatever my twenty-year-old self was, it was the pivot on which the circle of my life revolved. I do not think that I was a more selfish person than most. Through such unhappiness as I had known myself, I had a feeling for the unhappiness of others, and at least to those I liked I had it in me to be a good friend. But I was, as I have said, centered on myself. The tree, the cloud, the sun—I knew there was a wider world beyond myself and my small circle: the world that Saint Francis praised God for, the world that had marked with such sadness and pity and weariness the face of Jesus in Da Vinci's study. And I knew that somewhere out there, or deep beneath, there might well be God for all I knew. But all of that seemed very remote, mysterious and unreal compared with the immediate and absorbing reality of myself. And though I think I knew even then that finding that self and being that self and protecting and nurturing and enjoying that self was not the "everything" I called it in the poem, by and large it was everything that, to me, really mattered. That, in any event, was the surface I floated on and in many ways float on still as to one degree or another we all of us both do and must lest otherwise we get lost or drown in the depths. But to lose track of those depths to the extent that I was inclined to—to lose track of the deep needs beyond our own needs and those of our closest friends; to lose track of the deep mystery beyond or at the heart of the mystery of our separate selves—is to lose track also of what our journey is a journey toward and of the sacredness and high adventure of our journey. Nor, if we have our eyes, ears, hearts open at all, does life allow us to lose track of the depths for long.

When I got back to Princeton after the Army, for instance, the stream of things flowed on much as it had before, and I was carried along by the tumble of it. It was a wonderful time in many ways—the wonder of being my own person again, of wearing my own clothes instead of a uniform, of rediscovering old friends whom I had been sure I had lost forever. But I took my classes much more seriously than I had before because, after infiltration courses and German villages, they seemed a gift now instead of a drudgery, and in my reading I found my way somehow to some of the great prose writers of the seventeenth century—writers like Sir Thomas Browne and Bishop Jeremy Taylor and John Donne again, only as a preacher this time more than as a poet. No poetry I knew could match what seemed the great elegance and power of their prose. As usual, it was primarily their language that carried me away—the gorgeous latinate words, the stately cadences, the overladen sentences that wound their glittering, labyrinthine way across the page yet always came right at the end—but I could not entirely overlook the fact that what they were using their extraordinary language to describe was again and again their experience of the Extraordinary itself, and that this was the source as well as the subject of their unparalleled eloquence. It would be too much to say that I was converted by those men, but at the very least they made me prick up my ears, made me listen in a new way to what reverberated from beneath the surface of their words to give them such life.

"I shall rise from the dead," wrote John Donne,

Dean of Saint Paul's, "from the prostration, from the prosternation of death, and never miss the sun, which shall be put out, for I shall see the Son of God, the Sun of Glory, and shine myself as that sun shines. I shall rise from the grave, and never miss this city, which shall be nowhere, for I shall see the city of God, the new Jerusalem. I shall look up and never wonder when it shall be day, for the angel will tell me that time shall be no more, and I shall see and see cheerfully that last day of judgment, which shall have no night, never end, and be united to the Ancient of Days, to God himself, who had no morning, never began." I could not hear such passion in a human voice without catching some echo of it in myself, even though I was far from understanding more than a very little about what kind of passion it was or what effect it could have on a human life.

There were other voices, too. I was drinking beer with some friends at the Nassau Tavern again, that scene of an earlier epiphany, when in a fit of tipsy anger, boredom, bravado, one of them used the name of Jesus Christ in an oath of such blasphemy and obscenity that it shot me out of that place like an explosion. Into the darkness of the spring night I rode my bike down Nassau Street looking for a church that was open because, even full of beer as I was, I knew I had somehow to cleanse myself, cleanse Christ, make amends somehow not just for that one boy, but for the world itself, including me, for all the lostness and sadness and ugliness of us all. Every church I came to was bolted tight at that hour, but finally I found one where, by climbing up onto a stone balustrade, I was able at least to see the lighted altar inside and clung there to the chill stone until some kind of cleansing seemed to happen, some kind of amends made, if only within myself.

And during my senior year I started to write a novel. Its hero was a fat man named Tristram Bone, who was the lineal descendant, of course, of King Rinkitink and the Emperor Claudius and Louis the Sixteenth and the rest of them and who I have come more and more to believe, as I have occasionally thought about him since, was a kind of image not of myself as I was, but of myself as with some part of me I dreamed of being. I was on the thin side, actually, and in countless ways vulnerable, but he was fat, and his fatness seemed armor somehow against the perils of the world without and at the same time a powerful insulation against the fires that rage in the world within. He had somehow come out safe and at peace on the far side of something that I had scarcely even entered yet. He was optimistic and calm in the face of disaster whereas I, like my Grandmother Buechner before me, have always tended to imagine the worst in such killing detail that I mar even the fairest of my days with pointless worrying. He was by nature a compassionate doer of kind deeds whereas my own nature has always been—through diffidence and a sense of inadequacy as much as anything—to look the other way in the face of human need, so that such kindnesses as I have done in my life I have usually either had to force myself to do, or been forced by someone else, or have thought of as so alien to my nature that I have never been able very satisfactorily to take credit for them.

Beyond time is the phrase that I have used to describe this leg of my journey because it was then that I think I first began to have a pale version of the experience that Saint Paul describes in his letter to the Philippians. "Work out your own salvation with fear and trembling," he writes, "for God is at work in you both to will and to work for his good pleasure." I was a long way from thinking in terms of my own salvation or anybody else's, but through the people I met like the drunken boy at the Nass and the black man at the head of the line, through the courses I happened to take and the books I happened to read, through such events as eating that muddy turnip in Alabama, through my revulsion at my own weaknesses as well as through such satisfaction as I had in my own strengths, it seems to me now that a power from beyond time was working to achieve its own aim through my aimless life in time as it works through the lives of all of us and all our times.

Starting to write my first novel was part of it too, as have been all the novels I have written since, because what I developed through the writing of them was a sense of plot and, beyond that, a sense that perhaps life itself has a plot—that the events of our lives, random and witless as they generally seem, have a shape and direction of their own, are seeking to show us something, lead us somewhere. We are always free as in a way the characters in novels are also free—free to run away with the story, as the saying goes, free to be what they want to be no matter how hard the author may try to make them be something else—but in the midst of our freedom, we hear whispers from beyond time, I think, sense something hiddenly at work in all our working whose plot it is either for our sakes to make us truly and everlastingly human before it is done or, failing that and perhaps no less for our sakes, to let death be the merciful *coup de grâce* to our less-than-humanness. In any case, Tristram Bone, the hero of that earliest novel, appears on the first page seated in a barber chair facing the mirror in a white sheet that hangs from his shoulders like a robe. "The mirror reflected what seemed at first a priest," is the way the book begins, and insofar as what the mirror also reflected was an image, albeit an unconscious one, of myself, I cannot help thinking of that opening sentence as itself just such a whisper, as the first faint intimation from God knows where of the direction my life was even then starting to take me, although if anyone had said so at the time, I would have thought he was mad.

I choose to believe that, from beyond time, a saving mystery breaks into our time at odd and unforeseeable moments, and as I approach the end of this account of the early years of my journey, it is a few of those moments that I mainly want to describe. At the time that they occurred, I did not particularly mark them. A great many other things were happening that preoccupied me much more—things like graduating from Princeton, and taking my first job teaching English at Lawrenceville, and at the age of twenty, on the Saint Regis roof in New York, asking a girl to marry me who luckily for both of us said no; but in retrospect I can see that it was the beyond-time moments, inconsequential as they seemed by comparison, that counted for greatly more.

There was the day I signed the contract for that first novel that I had started in college, for instance. It was a major event for me, needless to say—the fulfillment of my wildest dreams of literary glory. But of the actual signing itself in the offices of Alfred Knopf—who was there and what was said and how I felt—I remember nothing. What I remember instead is leaving the publisher's office afterwards and running into somebody in the building whom I had known slightly at college. He was working as a messenger boy, he told me. I was, as I thought, on the brink of fame and fortune. But instead of feeling any pride or sense of superior accomplishment by the comparison, I remember a great and unheralded rush of something like sadness, almost like shame. I had been very lucky, and he had not been very lucky, and the pleasure that I might have taken in what had happened to me was all but lost in the realization that nothing comparable, as far as I could see, had happened to him. I wanted to say something or do something to make it up to him, but I had no idea how or what and ended up saying nothing of any consequence at all, least of all anything about the contract that I had just signed. We simply said good-bye in the lobby, he going his way and I mine, and that was that. All I can say now is that something small but unforgettable happened inside me as the result of that chance meeting—some small flickering out of the truth that, in the long run, there can be no real joy for anybody until there is joy finally for us all—and I can take no credit for it. It was nothing I piously thought my way to. It was no conscious attempt to work out my own salvation. What I felt was something better and truer than I was, or than I am, and it happened, as perhaps all such things do, as a gift.

The novel came out as *A Long Day's Dying* in January 1950, my second winter of teaching at Lawrenceville, and to my surprise as well as to the publisher's, it was immediately a considerable success both critically and commercially despite the fact that it was very dense, static, psychological, and written in such a mannered, involuted style—the residue of my romance with the seventeenth century—that it seems outrageous when I look at it now. "For Naya with love and wonder" was how I dedicated it, in partial payment of an ancient debt, and I put Naya herself in it as an old lady named Maroo, whose daughter Tristram Bone loves in his hopelessly ineffective and tongue-tied way. I also put a few other people in it whom I knew, setting it in Princeton, Tryon, and New York, but unlike many first novels, it was in no overt way autobiographical. Instead, like all the novels I have written since, it came from the same part of myself that dreams come from and by a process scarcely less obscure. I labor very hard at the actual writing of them, but the plot and characters and general feeling of them come from somewhere deeper down and farther away than conscious effort.

I took the title from a passage in *Paradise Lost* where Adam says to Eve that their expulsion from Paradise "will prove no sudden but a slow pac'd evil, / A long day's dying to augment our pain," and with the exception of the old lady Maroo, what all the characters seem to be dying of is loneliness, emptiness, sterility, and such preoccupation with themselves and their own problems that they are unable to communicate with each other about anything that really matters to them very much. I am sure that I chose such a melancholy theme partly because it seemed effective and fashionable, but I have no doubt that, like dreams generally, it also reflected the way I felt about at least some dimension of my own life and the lives of those around me. As I have said, the book turned out unaccountably to be a best-seller. It got my picture in the papers, in *Life* and *Time* and *Newsweek.* Clerks in bookshops recognized me from the photograph on the jacket, and I was more in the public eye then at the age of twenty-three than I have ever been again since. But the odd thing and the lucky thing is how little effect it had on me of the sort that might have been expected.

If I had been living in New York and trying to make my way primarily as a writer, I might easily have been caught up, I suppose, in living the kind of life that can turn people into celebrities if they are not careful, into people who, as somebody put it, become famous mainly just for being famous. There were parties I could have gone to, friendships I could have cultivated, other things I might have tried writing to dazzle the public eye while it was still so much on me. Moreover, with part of myself there was nothing that I would have loved better, and when I am feeling especially obscure and neglected as a writer I sometimes still think wistfully of how things might have turned out differently. But I was not living in New York. I was living in New Jersey. I was also teaching for the first time, and since I was only a year or two older than my oldest students, I had all I could do to keep ahead of them. Then, too, if there was something about being in the limelight that very much attracted me, there was also something in it that I recoiled from as involving too much of the same kind of emptiness I had described in my book. I was afraid, I think, of the person that I was—and to some degree, I suppose, always am— in danger of becoming. I also think that perhaps deep in me somewhere I was restrained by an echo of the revelation I had had the day I ran into my acquaintance at the publisher's: that in the last analysis, there is no fun in being famous unless everybody is famous.

I escaped all the ballyhoo relatively unscarred, in other words. The one mark it left on me, I think, was the feeling of being somehow special. The negative side of that feeling is plain enough. It was sheer ego. I had written a book that was compared with Henry James and Marcel Proust and, headier still, was labeled decadent. My unmemorable face and unpronounceable name had been in the papers. Strangers wrote me letters. The positive side was that this same sense of specialness made it very hard for me ever to settle for being anything less than special again. From that day to this I have been driven as a writer, and to a degree as a human being too, to write something, do something, be something to justify the fluke of that early and for the most part undeserved success. If that is not altogether what Saint Paul meant by working out your own salvation with fear and trembling, I suspect that it may be at least its second cousin.

And then, from wherever it is that they come from, there came another moment. Not long after *A Long Day's Dying* was published, a man I scarcely knew asked me to have lunch with him. He was one of the ministers who came regularly to preach at the Lawrenceville chapel and whose sermons had a sort of witty, sardonic liveliness to them. All through lunch I remember wondering why it was that he had sought me out. He was some twenty years older than I was, and we had nothing in common as far as I knew, had never exchanged more than a few words before. I have long since forgotten what we talked about, but it seems to me that he told me a good deal

8|952

about himself and his work, and I mainly just listened, drawing lines on the white table cloth with my fork as I wondered when he would get to the point if indeed there was any point. Then at some moment during the conversation, I became aware that the subject had switched from him to me. I was highly thought of as a writer, he said. There were a lot of people who took my words seriously and were influenced by them. Had I ever considered, he said—and though I cannot remember his words, I remember his tone of voice which was dry and slightly mocking in a way that left you uncertain whether it was you he was mocking or himself. He was a complicated sort of man with a little black moustache who spoke in a way that struck me as concealing more about him than it revealed. Had I ever considered, he said, putting my gift with words to work for—God, did he say? Or the Church? Or Christ? I no longer remember how he put it exactly, and he made no great thing of it but passed on soon to other matters so that I do not to this day know whether this was what he had asked me to lunch to say or not. I no longer remember what I answered him either or what impression his words made on me except that they took me entirely by surprise. No, I must have told him. I had never considered such a thing. And that was the end of it except that out of all the events that took place during those five years of teaching at Lawrenceville, it is one of the few that I remember distinctly, like an old photograph preserved by accident between the pages of a book.

I remember, too, the terror and delight of teaching back there in my old school so soon after graduating from it myself. The terror was that someday in the middle of a sentence I would simply run out of things to say, and the class would rise up and denounce me for the impostor that in my heart I knew I was. And the delight of it was that if things ever somehow catch fire in a class, something happens in the air between master and students that is so much better and wiser and more alive than any of them that every distinction between who is taught and who is teaching all but vanishes. And there was the strange delight, too, of finding myself suddenly the colleague of men who had so recently been my mentors and heroes. It was by no means easy at first, but little by little Mr. Martin became Dick, and Mr. Thurber Gerrish, and even the olympian Mr. Heely an always somewhat precarious Allan, as fathers turned into brothers and brothers into friends.

Then one weekend I went to a monastery, the Order of the Holy Cross in West Park, New York, on the Hudson river. I do not know why it is that we remember so much about some of the small decisions of our lives and so little about most of the great ones, but for me at least that has always tended to be the case. Maybe it is because the great decisions are not made at some particular moment in time but deep within us have been so long in the making that we find ourselves acting on them before we are altogether conscious of having decided to. As nearly as I can recall, I had two reasons for going. One of them was that I had heard that one of the monks there was a man of great wisdom and sanctity, and I had questions I wanted to ask him which I have long since forgotten just as I would undoubtedly have long since forgotten his answers. The other reason was that I felt I needed somehow to be cleansed of the too-muchness and too-littleness of my life, to be cleansed as much as anything, I suppose, of myself. I have already described the experience in some detail elsewhere, so all I will say here is that in most ways it was a flop. The monk I had come to see had taken on some special vows and could not be seen, and all the other monks practiced the vow of silence except for one elderly one, known as the Guest Master, who had the responsibility of talking to visitors like me, but as the result of a stroke spoke so indistinctly as to be almost unintelligible. So none of my questions was answered, whatever they were. I met no one who gave me whatever help I had come for or whom I ever saw again or especially wanted to. Nothing in that sense happened. But silence happened—silence at meals, in corridors, the silence of men who for the love of God kept silent; and to some degree silence happened also in myself, silence not merely as the absence of speech but as a kind of speech itself or at least as a prelude to speech, a prelude to hearing someone or something speak out of the silence.

When it came time for me to leave after a couple of days, the Guest Master asked if I would like him to hear my confession, and I cringed with embarrassment. I told him I thought you confessed your sins to God. Well, but sometimes it meant more to confess them to God through a priest, he said. So I told him what I could, told a few of the things I had done that I thought were sinful —childish, fleshly things for the most part, but terrible to tell—and at the end I suppose he must have pronounced my forgiveness, though I do not remember feeling particularly forgiven or cleansed. But the old man himself

I remember, some special combination of sternness and kindness about him. Would I like him to give me his blessing, he asked? And as much out of politeness as anything, and because I thought that then maybe he would let me go, I said yes, so he indicated that I was to kneel, and down on the stone floor I knelt, as awkwardly as I had confessed, if not more so, and he signed me with the cross and blessed me. "You have a long way to go," he said, his only words that I think I remember exactly. I had a long way to go.

"My own heart let me more have pity on," Gerard Manley Hopkins wrote in the sonnet I have already quoted from, and then he goes on: "Leave comfort root-room; let joy size / At God knows when to God knows what; whose smile / 's not wrung, see you: unforeseen times rather." Nor is it only the joy of God and the comfort of God that come at unforeseen times. God's coming is always unforeseen, I think, and the reason, if I had to guess, is that if he gave us anything much in the way of advance warning, more often than not we would have made ourselves scarce long before he got there.

One evening toward the end of my five years of teaching, for instance, what I thought was coming was just dinner with my mother. She was living by herself in New York at the time, and it must have been some sort of occasion, I think, because the apartment looked unusually nice, and there were candles on the table, the best silver. It was to be just the two of us, and we had both looked forward to it, not simply as mother and son but as two old friends who no longer got to see each other all that much. Then, just as we were about to sit down to eat, the telephone rang, and it was for me. It was a friend I taught with at Lawrenceville, and he had not spoken more than a word or two when his voice broke and I realized to my horror that he was weeping. His mother and father and a pregnant sister had been in an automobile accident on the West Coast, and it was uncertain whether any of them would live. He was at the airport waiting for a flight to take him out to them. Could I come down, he asked, and wait with him till the plane left?

There are many people in this world—I suspect they may even be in the majority—who in face of such a cry for help as that would have seen right away that, humanly speaking, there was no alternative but to say that they would be at the airport as soon as a taxi would take them there. I have known many such people in my day and can explain them only on the grounds that they are strong, compassionate, and at least in that sense, Christian by instinct. My instinct, on the other hand, was to be nothing so much as afraid. I was afraid of my friend's fear and of his tears. I was afraid of his faith that I could somehow be a comfort and help to him and afraid that I was not friend enough to be able to be. Dating perhaps from that November morning of my childhood when I opened the door of Jamie's and my bedroom on a tragic and terrifying world that I had no resources for dealing with, I was afraid of opening the door into his pain or anybody's pain. So although I knew as well as anybody that I had no choice but to say that I would come, what I said instead, Heaven help me, was that I would come if I possibly could but there were things I had to take care of first and would he phone me back in about ten minutes.

In the other room dinner was on the table and my mother was waiting, and on that placid stage there was played out a preposterous little scene that was nonetheless one of the watersheds of my life. Because when I told my mother what had happened and that I was probably going to have to leave and skip supper, her reaction caught me completely off guard. The whole thing was absurd, she said. My friend was a grown man. He had no business carrying on like a hysterical child. What earthly good could I do anyway? It was outrageous to think of spoiling an evening together that we had both been looking forward to for days. Everything she said was precisely what at some level of my being I had already been saying to myself, and that was of course what made it so appalling. It was only when I heard it on someone else's lips that I heard it for what it was, and as much out of revulsion at myself as out of pity for my friend, I resolved that as soon as he called again, I would tell him that I would come immediately.

Then, as the final absurdity, when he did call again, he said that he had gotten hold of himself and there was really no longer any need for me to come at all, and the consequence was that I did not go, did not go, and such as it was my mother and I had our evening together after all. But in the long run the consequences went much farther than that because if the result of opening that November door some seventeen years earlier was that time started for me, and my journey through time, the result of that phone call and of my response to it was the start of another kind of journey altogether, the journey that the old monk referred to when he said I had a long way to go. My mother's apartment by candlelight was haven and home and shelter from everything in the world that seemed dangerous and a threat to my peace. And my friend's broken voice on the phone was a voice calling me out into that dangerous world not simply for his sake, as I suddenly saw it, but also for my sake. The shattering revelation of that moment was that true peace, the high and bidding peace that passeth all understanding, is to be had not in retreat from the battle, but only in the thick of the battle. To journey for the sake of saving our own lives is little by little to cease to live in any sense that really matters, even to ourselves, because it is only by journeying for the world's sake—even when the world bores and sickens and scares you half to death —that little by little we start to come alive. It was not a conclusion that I came to in time. It was a conclusion from beyond time that came to me. God knows I have never been any good at following the road it pointed me to, but at least, by grace, I glimpsed the road and saw that it is the only one worth traveling.

What followed can be quickly told although it was not so quickly lived. After five years of teaching and the publication of a second novel that fared as badly as the first one had fared well, I gave up my Lawrenceville job and in 1953 went to New York to be a full-time writer, only to discover that I could not write a word. So I decided that maybe I should try to make money instead and went to see a former partner of my uncle about the possibility of going into the advertising business; but he said that although there was plenty of money to be made there, you had to have a very tough hide to survive, and

I decided that probably my hide was not tough enough. So I turned to the CIA, of all things, thinking that if there was going to be another war, I would probably stand a better chance of surviving as a spy than back in the infantry again; but when I was asked by an interviewer in Washington if I would be willing to submit a person to physical torture in order to extract information that many lives might depend on, I decided that I had no stomach for that either, and another road was barred. And somewhere in the process I fell in love again with a girl who did not fall in love with me. It all sounds like a kind of inane farce as I set it down here, with every door I tried to open slammed on my foot, and yet I suppose it was also a kind of pilgrim's progress. I suppose, too, that when you get right down to the flesh and blood of things, the pilgrimage and the farce always go hand in hand because it is a divine comedy that we are all of us involved in after all, not a divine dirge, and when Saint Paul calls us to be fools for Christ, it is not to frock coats and poke bonnets that he is calling us, but to motley and a cap with bells.

Part of the farce was that for the first time in my life that year in New York, I started going to church regularly, and what was farcical about it was not that I went but my reason for going, which was simply that on the same block where I lived there happened to be a church with a preacher I had heard of and that I had nothing all that much better to do with my lonely Sundays. The preacher was a man named George Buttrick, and Sunday after Sunday I went, and sermon after sermon I heard. It was not just his eloquence that kept me coming back, though he was wonderfully eloquent, literate, imaginative, never letting you guess what he was going to come out with next but twitching with surprises up there in the pulpit, his spectacles a-glitter in the lectern light. What drew me more was whatever it was that his sermons came from and whatever it was in me that they touched so deeply. And then there came one particular sermon with one particular phrase in it that does not even appear in a transcript of his words that somebody sent me more than twenty-five years later so I can only assume that he must have dreamed it up at the last minute and ad-libbed it—and on just such foolish, tenuous, holy threads as that, I suppose, hang the destinies of us all. Jesus Christ refused the crown that Satan offered him in the wilderness, Buttrick said, but he is king nonetheless because again and again he is crowned in the heart of the people who believe in him. And that inward coronation takes place, Buttrick said, "among confession, and tears, and great laughter."

It was the phrase *great laughter* that did it, did whatever it was that I believe must have been hiddenly in the doing all the years of my journey up till then. It was not so much that a door opened as that I suddenly found that a door had been open all along which I had only just then stumbled upon. After church, with a great lump still in my throat, I walked up to 84th Street to have Sunday dinner with Grandma Buechner. She sat in her usual chair with the little Philco silent at her side and a glass of sherry in her hand, and when I told her something of what had happened, I could see that she was as much bemused as pleased by what I had said. I have forgotten her words, but the sense of her answer was that she was happy for me that I had found whatever it was that I had found. *Le bon Dieu.* You could never be sure what he was up to. If there was a *bon Dieu* at all. Who could say? Then old Rosa came listing in to say *Essen ist fertig, Frau Büchner,* and we went in to lunch.

Whatever it was that I had found. Whoever it was. The painting in the book. The recurring reference in those early, embarrassing poems. The name on the lips of the beery boy at the Nass. The priest trudging down the sun-drenched Bermuda lane, and the man with the beard who met all the ships when they docked and searched all the faces. The crowing of the rooster and the sound of voices I could not quite make out in another room, and the sound of my friend's voice on the phone that I could make out all too well. My father's writing on the last page of *Gone with the Wind* that he was no good, and then, because he believed that, giving his life away for what he must have thought was our good and thus in his own sad, lost way echoing with his unimaginable gift another holy gift more unimaginable still. What I found was what I had already half seen, or less than half, in many places over my twenty-seven years without ever clearly knowing what it was that I was seeing or even that I was seeing anything of great importance. Something in me recoils from using such language, but here at the end I am left with no other way of saying it than that what I found finally was Christ. Or was found. It hardly seems to matter which. There are other words for describing what happened to me—psychological words, historical words, poetic words—but in honesty as well as in faith I am reduced to the word that is his name because no other seems to account for the experience so fully.

To say that I was born again, to use that traditional phrase, is to say too much because I remained in most ways as self-centered and squeamish after the fact as I was before, and God knows remain so still. And in another way to say that I was born again is to say too little because there have been more than a few such moments since, times when from beyond time something too precious to tell has glinted in the dusk, always just out of reach, like fireflies.

I went to see Buttrick himself the week after his sermon and told him that I found myself wondering if maybe I should go to a seminary to discover more about whatever it was that seemed to have taken place and what I should do about it, and after he asked me a few questions and pointed out that there were various roads open to me, what he did was this. He was a busy man in charge of a big and busy church, but he took his hat and coat out of the closet, handed me mine, and then drove me in his car from Madison Avenue at 73rd Street to Union Theological Seminary at Broadway and 120th Street, where I eventually entered as a student the following fall.

That made a journey of forty-seven blocks all told, not counting the long crosstown blocks at the top of the park. It was a long way to go, and there is no question but that there is a vastly longer way to go still, for all of us, before we are done. And the way we have to go is full of perils, both from without and from within, and who can say for sure what we will find at the end of our journeys, or if, when that time comes, it will prove to be anything more than such a beautiful dream as Caliban dreamed. But here at the last I find myself thinking about

King Rinkitink again—another king strong in his weakness and stout of heart in the face of despair—and of those three pearls that he carried with him. The blue one that conferred such strength that no one could resist it. The pink one that protected its owner from all dangers. And the pure white one that spoke wisdom.

Faith. Hope. Love. Those are their names of course, those three—as words so worn out, but as realities so rich. Our going-away presents from beyond time to carry with us through time to lighten our step as we go. And part at least of the wisdom of the third one is, as Rinkitink heard it, "Never question the truth of what you fail to understand, for the world is filled with wonders." Above all, never question the truth beyond all understanding and surpassing all other wonders that in the long run nothing, not even the world, not even ourselves, can separate us forever from that last and deepest love that glimmers in our dusk like a pearl, like a face.